THIS BOOK

BELONGS TO

....

....

I know you could have picked from many other books, but you chose this one. So, a big thanks for reading all the way to the end. If you enjoyed this book or received value from it, I'd like to ask you for a favor. Please take a few minutes to **post an honest and heartfelt review on** Amazon.com. Your support does make a difference and helps to benefit other people.

Thanks!

Table of Contents

Introduction   27

What is Self-Discipline?   29

    Self-Discipline: A Misunderstood Power   29

    Self-Discipline Begins in the Mind   30

    Self-Discipline and Willpower   31

    Mental Toughness and Character   33

The Psychology of Self-Discipline   34

Immerse Yourself in the Culture of Self-Discipline   38

    Surround Yourself with Disciplined People   38

The Power of Self-Discipline   42

Building Mental Toughness   48

    The Mental Toughness of Soldiers   48

    Who Exhibits Mental Toughness?   49

    Daily Practices for Mental Toughness   51

    Four mental toughness techniques inspired by war   54

How to Apply Self-Discipline in Your Life   59

Consistency and How to Develop Positive Habits   65

Persistence Is the Key to Self-Discipline   69

Self-Discipline and Happiness   75

Self-Discipline and Living in the Moment   81

Understanding Your Personality   86

Its Goal Setting Time!   90

    Setting Your Goals   92

    Strategies to Help You Achieve the Goals You Set   95

Organization as A Form of Discipline   97

Time Management   101

The Strength to Say NO!   105

How to Maintain Self-Discipline when Facing Adversity   107

    Eliminate excuses   108

    The Importance Of Avoiding Perfectionism And Procrastination   109

    Keep everything simple   111

Make things fun   113

Challenges and Setbacks   115

Pride   120

Conclusion   122

SUMMARY

The Power of Self-Discipline is a concept that holds immense significance in various aspects of life. It refers to the ability to control and regulate one's thoughts, actions, and behaviors in order to achieve desired goals and outcomes. Self-discipline is not an innate trait but rather a skill that can be developed and honed through consistent practice and conscious effort.

In today's fast-paced and highly competitive world, self-discipline has become more crucial than ever. It is the driving force behind personal and professional success, as it enables individuals to stay focused, motivated, and committed to their objectives. Whether it is in the realm of academics, career, relationships, or personal growth, self-discipline plays a pivotal role in determining the level of achievement and fulfillment one can attain.

One of the key benefits of self-discipline is its ability to enhance productivity and efficiency. By cultivating self-discipline, individuals are able to prioritize tasks, manage their time effectively, and avoid distractions. This allows them to make the most of their resources and accomplish more in less time. Moreover, self-discipline helps in developing a strong work ethic, which is essential for long-term success and career advancement.

Self-discipline also plays a crucial role in maintaining good physical and mental health. It enables individuals to adopt healthy habits such as regular exercise, balanced diet, and adequate sleep. By practicing self-discipline in these areas, individuals can improve their overall well-being, boost their energy levels, and reduce the risk of various health issues. Additionally, self-discipline helps in managing stress and anxiety, as it allows individuals to stay calm, composed, and focused even in challenging situations.

Furthermore, self-discipline is closely linked to personal growth and self-improvement. It requires individuals to step out of their comfort zones, overcome obstacles, and push themselves beyond their limits. By consistently practicing self-discipline, individuals can develop new skills, acquire knowledge, and expand their horizons. This not only leads to personal growth but also opens up new opportunities and possibilities for success.

In conclusion, the power of self-discipline cannot be underestimated. It is a fundamental attribute that enables individuals to achieve their goals, excel in their endeavors, and lead a fulfilling life. By cultivating self-discipline, individuals can enhance their productivity, maintain good health, and foster personal growth. It is a skill that can be learned and mastered, and its benefits are boundless. Therefore, it is essential for individuals to recognize the importance of self-discipline

Self-discipline is a crucial trait that plays a significant role in shaping an individual's success and overall well-being. It refers to the ability to control one's impulses, emotions, and behaviors in order to achieve long-term goals and maintain a sense of self-control. While it may seem challenging to practice self-discipline consistently, its importance cannot be overstated.

One of the primary reasons why self-discipline matters is that it enables individuals to overcome procrastination and stay focused on their goals. In today's fast-paced world, distractions are abundant, and it is easy to get sidetracked by various temptations and instant gratifications. However, those who possess self-discipline are able to resist these distractions and stay committed to their objectives. They understand the value of delayed gratification and are willing to put in the necessary effort and time to achieve their desired outcomes.

Moreover, self-discipline is closely linked to personal growth and development. By practicing self-discipline, individuals are able to establish healthy habits and routines that contribute to their overall well-being. Whether it is maintaining a regular exercise routine, sticking to a balanced diet, or dedicating time to personal and professional development, self-discipline allows individuals to make consistent progress towards their goals. It helps in cultivating a strong work ethic and a sense of responsibility, which are essential qualities for success in any area of life.

Self-discipline also plays a crucial role in managing stress and overcoming challenges. Life is full of obstacles and setbacks, and it is during these difficult times that self-discipline becomes even more important. It helps individuals to stay calm, focused, and resilient in the face of adversity. By maintaining self-discipline, individuals are able to persevere through tough times, learn from their failures, and bounce back stronger than before.

Furthermore, self-discipline is closely tied to building and maintaining healthy relationships. It allows individuals to exercise self-control in their interactions with others, avoiding impulsive reactions and conflicts. By practicing self-discipline, individuals are able to communicate effectively, listen attentively, and empathize with others. This fosters trust, respect, and understanding in relationships, leading to stronger connections and a more harmonious social environment.

In conclusion, self-discipline is a fundamental trait that is essential for personal growth, success, and overall well-being. It enables individuals to overcome procrastination, stay focused on their goals, and establish healthy habits. It also helps in managing stress, overcoming challenges, and building and maintaining healthy relationships.

Self-discipline can be defined as the ability to control one's own behavior, thoughts, and emotions in order to achieve specific goals or adhere to a set of principles or values. It involves making conscious choices and taking deliberate actions that align with one's long-term objectives, even in the face of distractions, temptations, or difficulties.

At its core, self-discipline is about having the willpower and inner strength to resist immediate gratification or short-term pleasures in favor of long-term rewards or personal growth. It requires individuals to prioritize their goals and make sacrifices in the present moment for the sake of future success or fulfillment.

Self-discipline encompasses various aspects of life, including physical health, mental well-being, personal relationships, and professional development. In terms of physical health, it involves maintaining a balanced diet, engaging in regular exercise, getting enough sleep, and avoiding harmful habits such as smoking or excessive alcohol consumption. It also entails practicing self-care and prioritizing mental well-being through activities like meditation, journaling, or seeking therapy when needed.

In personal relationships, self-discipline involves being mindful of one's words and actions, showing empathy and understanding towards others, and practicing effective communication and conflict resolution skills. It requires individuals to resist the urge to react impulsively or engage in harmful behaviors that may damage relationships or cause emotional harm to others.

In the professional realm, self-discipline is crucial for achieving career success and personal growth. It involves setting clear goals, managing time effectively, staying focused on tasks, and consistently putting in the effort required to excel in one's chosen field. It also entails being proactive, taking initiative, and continuously seeking opportunities for learning and improvement.

Developing self-discipline is not always easy, as it requires individuals to overcome their own weaknesses, break bad habits, and push through discomfort or challenges. However, it is a skill that can be cultivated and strengthened over time through consistent practice and self-reflection. Strategies for enhancing self-discipline include setting specific and realistic goals, creating a structured routine, breaking tasks into smaller, manageable steps, seeking support from others, and celebrating small victories along the way.

In conclusion, self-discipline is a fundamental trait that enables individuals to take control of their lives, make intentional choices, and work towards their desired outcomes. It is a key ingredient for personal and professional success, as it empowers individuals to overcome obstacles, stay focused, and persevere in the pursuit of their goals.

The Psychology of Self-Discipline is a fascinating and complex topic that delves into the inner workings of the human mind and its ability to control and regulate behavior. Self-discipline refers to the ability to resist immediate gratification and instead focus on long-term goals and objectives. It involves making conscious choices and exerting self-control to overcome temptations and distractions.

Understanding the psychology behind self-discipline is crucial for individuals who wish to improve their ability to stay focused, motivated, and achieve their desired outcomes. It involves exploring various psychological factors that influence self-discipline, such as motivation, willpower, self-control, and goal-setting.

Motivation plays a significant role in self-discipline. It is the driving force that compels individuals to take action and persevere in the face of challenges. Motivation can be intrinsic, stemming from personal values, desires, and aspirations, or extrinsic, driven by external rewards or consequences. Understanding what motivates us and aligning our goals with our values can enhance our self-discipline.

Willpower is another crucial aspect of self-discipline. It refers to the ability to resist short-term temptations and impulses in favor of long-term goals. Willpower can be thought of as a mental muscle that can be strengthened through practice and training. However, it is also a limited resource that can be depleted over time, making it important to manage and replenish it effectively.

Self-control is closely related to willpower and involves regulating one's thoughts, emotions, and behaviors. It requires individuals to be aware of their impulses and consciously choose to act in alignment with their goals. Developing self-control involves practicing mindfulness, emotional regulation, and impulse control techniques.

Goal-setting is a fundamental aspect of self-discipline. Setting clear, specific, and achievable goals provides individuals with a sense of direction and purpose. Goals act as a roadmap, guiding individuals towards their desired outcomes and helping them stay focused and motivated. Breaking down larger goals into smaller, manageable tasks can also enhance self-discipline by providing a sense of progress and accomplishment.

In addition to these psychological factors, there are various strategies and techniques that can be employed to improve self-discipline. These include creating a supportive environment, developing effective time management skills, practicing self-reflection and self-awareness, seeking social support, and utilizing rewards and incentives.

Overall, the psychology of self-discipline is a multifaceted field that encompasses various psychological factors, strategies, and techniques. By understanding and harnessing these elements, individuals can

Self-discipline and willpower are often used interchangeably, but they are actually two distinct concepts with subtle differences. While both

involve the ability to control one's actions and impulses, self-discipline refers to the practice of consistently adhering to a set of rules or principles, while willpower refers to the ability to resist short-term temptations or impulses in order to achieve long-term goals.

Self-discipline is a broader concept that encompasses various aspects of one's life. It involves setting clear goals, establishing routines, and consistently following through with actions that align with those goals. Self-discipline requires a strong sense of commitment and determination to stay focused and motivated, even when faced with obstacles or distractions. It involves making conscious choices and sacrifices in order to prioritize long-term success over immediate gratification.

On the other hand, willpower is more specific and relates to the ability to resist immediate temptations or impulses that may hinder progress towards a goal. It is often described as a mental muscle that can be strengthened through practice. Willpower is particularly important when faced with situations that require delayed gratification, such as resisting unhealthy food choices or avoiding procrastination. It involves exerting self-control and making conscious decisions to override momentary desires in favor of long-term benefits.

While self-discipline and willpower are distinct, they are closely intertwined and often work in tandem. Self-discipline provides the foundation for developing willpower, as it involves creating a structure and routine that supports the pursuit of long-term goals. Willpower, on the other hand, acts as a tool within self-discipline, enabling individuals to resist immediate temptations and stay on track.

It is important to note that both self-discipline and willpower can be developed and strengthened over time. They are not fixed traits that some individuals possess inherently, but rather skills that can be cultivated through practice and conscious effort. Strategies such as setting specific goals, breaking them down into manageable steps, and rewarding oneself for progress can help enhance self-discipline and willpower.

In conclusion, while self-discipline and willpower are often used interchangeably, they are distinct concepts that play different roles in achieving personal goals. Self-discipline involves consistently adhering to a set of principles and routines, while willpower refers to the ability to resist immediate temptations. Both are essential for long-term success and can be developed through practice and conscious effort.

Intrinsic motivation refers to the internal drive and desire to engage in an activity or pursue a goal for its own sake, without any external rewards or incentives. It is driven by personal enjoyment, interest, and satisfaction derived from the activity itself. Intrinsic motivation is often associated with a sense of autonomy, competence, and personal growth. People who are intrinsically motivated are more likely to engage in activities willingly and persistently, as they find them inherently fulfilling and meaningful.

On the other hand, extrinsic motivation involves engaging in an activity or pursuing a goal primarily for external rewards or incentives, such as money, recognition, or praise. It is driven by the desire to obtain something external or avoid negative consequences. Extrinsic motivation can be effective in certain situations, especially when there is a clear link between the behavior and the desired outcome. However, it may not be as sustainable or fulfilling in the long run, as the focus is primarily on the external rewards rather than the inherent enjoyment or satisfaction derived from the activity itself.

Both intrinsic and extrinsic motivation play important roles in shaping human behavior and driving performance. While intrinsic motivation is often considered more desirable and beneficial, as it fosters a sense of autonomy and personal fulfillment, extrinsic motivation can also be effective in certain contexts. For example, in a work setting, extrinsic rewards such as bonuses or promotions can provide a sense of recognition and achievement, which can motivate employees to perform at their best.

It is important to note that the distinction between intrinsic and extrinsic motivation is not always clear-cut, as individuals may experience a combination of both types of motivation in different situations. Additionally, the same activity or goal can be driven by different motivations for different individuals. Understanding the underlying motivations can help individuals and organizations design strategies and environments that foster motivation and engagement.

Using Motivation as a Catalyst for Self-Discipline: Unlocking Your Full Potential

Introduction:

Self-discipline is a crucial trait that enables individuals to achieve their goals and lead a successful life. It involves the ability to control one's impulses, stay focused, and consistently work towards desired outcomes. While self-discipline is often seen as a challenging skill to develop, motivation can serve as a powerful catalyst in cultivating and sustaining this trait. By understanding the relationship between motivation and self-discipline, individuals can unlock their full potential and accomplish remarkable feats.

Understanding Motivation:

Motivation is the driving force behind our actions and behaviors. It is the internal or external stimulus that compels us to act in a certain way. Motivation can stem from various sources, such as personal goals, rewards, recognition, or even the desire to avoid negative consequences. When we are motivated, we experience a surge of energy and enthusiasm, which propels us towards taking action.

The Role of Motivation in Self-Discipline:

Motivation acts as a catalyst for self-discipline by providing the initial spark and sustaining the momentum required to stay on track. It serves as a reminder of why we started on a particular path and helps us overcome obstacles and setbacks along the way. Without motivation, self-discipline can waver, making it difficult to maintain consistency and focus.

Setting Clear Goals:

Motivation and self-discipline work hand in hand when it comes to goal setting. Clear and specific goals provide a sense of direction and purpose, which in turn fuels motivation. When we have a clear vision of what we want to achieve, we are more likely to stay disciplined and committed to the necessary actions. Motivation acts as a constant reminder of the rewards and benefits that await us upon achieving our goals, further strengthening our self-discipline.

Creating a Supportive Environment:

Motivation can also be enhanced by creating a supportive environment. Surrounding ourselves with like-minded individuals who share similar goals and aspirations can provide the necessary encouragement and accountability. Additionally, eliminating distractions and creating a conducive workspace can help maintain focus and discipline. By consciously designing our environment to align with our goals, we can boost our motivation and reinforce self-discipline.

Building Momentum:

Motivation can be harnessed to build momentum in our pursuit of self-discipline. Starting with small, achievable tasks and gradually increasing the level of difficulty can help create a sense of progress and accomplishment. Each small success fuels motivation, making it easier to tackle more challenging tasks.

The role of the environment in self-discipline is a crucial aspect that significantly influences an individual's ability to maintain self-control and adhere to their goals and commitments. The environment encompasses various external factors, such as physical surroundings, social influences, and personal habits, which can either facilitate or hinder the development and practice of self-discipline.

Firstly, the physical surroundings play a significant role in shaping an individual's self-discipline. A well-organized and clutter-free environment can promote focus and concentration, enabling individuals to stay on track with their tasks and goals. On the other hand, a chaotic and disorganized environment can create distractions and temptations, making it more challenging to maintain self-discipline. For instance, a messy workspace with numerous distractions, such as a television or social media notifications, can divert an individual's attention and hinder their ability to stay disciplined.

Secondly, social influences within the environment can greatly impact an individual's self-discipline. The people we surround ourselves with can either support or undermine our efforts to maintain self-control. Being in the company of disciplined and motivated individuals can inspire and encourage us to stay on track with our goals. Conversely, being surrounded by individuals who lack self-discipline or engage in unhealthy habits can make it more difficult to resist temptations and maintain our own self-discipline. Therefore, it is essential to choose our social circle wisely and seek out individuals who share similar values and goals.

Furthermore, personal habits and routines also play a crucial role in self-discipline. The environment we create for ourselves through our daily habits and routines can either foster or hinder our ability to practice self-discipline. Establishing consistent routines, such as waking up early, exercising regularly, and setting specific times for work or study, can help create a structured environment that promotes self-discipline. Additionally, cultivating healthy habits, such as proper nutrition, adequate sleep, and regular breaks, can provide the necessary physical and mental energy to sustain self-discipline.

In conclusion, the role of the environment in self-discipline cannot be underestimated. The physical surroundings, social influences, and personal habits all contribute to an individual's ability to maintain self-control and adhere to their goals and commitments. By creating an environment that supports focus, surrounding oneself with disciplined individuals, and cultivating healthy habits, individuals can enhance their self-discipline and increase their chances of achieving success in various aspects of life.

Procrastination is a common behavior that many individuals struggle with, and understanding the triggers behind this behavior can be crucial in overcoming it. Procrastination refers to the act of delaying or postponing tasks or actions that need to be completed, often resulting in increased stress, decreased productivity, and missed deadlines. While it may seem like a simple act of laziness or lack of motivation, there are actually various underlying factors that contribute to procrastination.

One of the main triggers of procrastination is fear of failure. Many individuals tend to put off tasks or projects because they are afraid of not meeting expectations or making mistakes. This fear can be paralyzing and prevent individuals from even starting a task, as they anticipate negative outcomes. The fear of failure can stem from various sources, such as past experiences of criticism or rejection, perfectionism, or a lack of self-confidence. Understanding and addressing these underlying fears is essential in overcoming procrastination.

Another common trigger of procrastination is a lack of clarity or direction. When individuals are unsure about how to approach a task or what steps to take, they may feel overwhelmed and choose to delay starting it. This lack of clarity can be due to a lack of knowledge or skills, uncertainty about priorities, or a lack of a clear plan. Breaking down tasks into smaller, manageable steps and seeking guidance or support from others can help alleviate this trigger and provide a sense of direction.

Additionally, procrastination can be triggered by a lack of motivation or interest in the task at hand. When individuals do not find a task engaging or meaningful, they may struggle to find the drive to start or complete it. This lack of motivation can be influenced by various factors, such as a mismatch between personal values and the task, a lack of intrinsic rewards, or a feeling of being overwhelmed by the effort required. Finding ways to make tasks more enjoyable or meaningful, setting clear goals and rewards, and finding personal connections to the task can help increase motivation and reduce procrastination.

Furthermore, external factors can also contribute to procrastination. Distractions, such as social media, television, or other forms of entertainment, can easily divert individuals' attention away from their tasks. Procrastination can also be triggered by a lack of structure or accountability, as individuals may feel less motivated to complete tasks when there are no external deadlines or consequences. Creating a conducive environment for productivity, setting specific deadlines, and seeking external support or accountability can help mitigate these external triggers.

Starting your self-discipline journey can be both exciting and challenging. It requires a strong commitment and a willingness to push yourself outside of your comfort zone. However, the rewards that come from developing self-discipline are truly worth the effort.

One of the first steps in embarking on your self-discipline journey is to set clear and achievable goals. These goals should be specific, measurable, attainable, relevant, and time-bound (SMART). By having a clear vision of what you want to achieve, you can create a roadmap that will guide you towards success.

Once you have set your goals, it is important to create a plan of action. This plan should outline the steps you need to take in order to reach your goals. Breaking down your goals into smaller, manageable tasks can make them feel less overwhelming and more attainable. By taking consistent action towards your goals, you will build momentum and develop the habit of self-discipline.

Another crucial aspect of self-discipline is managing your time effectively. Time management skills are essential for staying focused and avoiding distractions. Prioritizing your tasks and creating a schedule can help you make the most of your time and ensure that you are dedicating enough energy to your self-discipline journey.

In addition to managing your time, it is important to take care of your physical and mental well-being. Self-discipline requires mental strength and resilience, so it is important to prioritize self-care activities such as exercise, healthy eating, and getting enough sleep. Taking care of your physical health will provide you with the energy and mental clarity needed to stay disciplined and focused.

It is also important to surround yourself with a supportive network of individuals who share your goals and values. Having a support system can provide you with encouragement, accountability, and motivation during challenging times. Whether it is joining a self-discipline group or finding a mentor, having others who understand and support your journey can make a significant difference in your success.

Lastly, it is important to remember that self-discipline is a lifelong journey. It is not something that can be achieved overnight, but rather a skill that needs to be continuously practiced and developed. There will be times when you may stumble or face setbacks, but it is important to stay committed and persevere. Each setback is an opportunity for growth and learning.

Introduction

This book aims to help you live your life in general in a more disciplined way. Discipline is not just for children; growing up and becoming adults does not automatically make them more disciplined. Discipline is not synonymous with punishment, punishment or severity. It is possible for anyone to become a disciple of the discipline.

Take an analysis of yourself before anything else. Try to understand what are the obstacles that stand between you and your desire to be more disciplined. These barriers can consist of defects of character, an inability to articulate what you want from life or a dependency on stimulants or other drugs. Perhaps, try to conform to the rules without ever thinking about yourself; this could make it easy for you to adapt to the idea of discipline that someone else has without pausing to think about what kind of discipline is best suited to you and which you may need for your needs. Whatever the reason, try to find out before proceeding.

Why do you feel you do not have self-disciplined enough now? What prevents you from getting better?

In addition to evaluating your limits, consider how the people around you affect you. Do you spend too much time pleasing others and you never think of yourself? Do you always give in to the demands of others and have you put your needs in obscurity?

Try to convince yourself that you need to be more disciplined to be able to believe in yourself. Doing so will be indispensable in particular if you spend a lot of time trying to please others. It will be much difficult for you to be disciplined if you think it is necessary for others to have limits, set boundaries, tell you how to act, think or behave.

What voices in your head tell you that you are a failure or a real failure? These are negative thoughts that have no basis and must be addressed so that you can begin to take care of yourself and live in a more disciplined way. You may need to go into therapy or perhaps it would be enough for you to process your negative thoughts by being aware of their existence, or by using cognitive behavioral techniques.

Choose a sphere in which you want to be more disciplined. In which sphere of life do you want more rigor? Perhaps it is about work, study, keeping a clean-living room or doing without a bad habit, etc.

What is Self-Discipline?

Self-discipline is a learned behavior; no one is born being self-disciplined. Like any other skill, self-discipline needs to be cultivated. It is the fruit that is yielded when we learn how to effectively challenge ourselves and experience the deeper inner potential that lies within us. Self-discipline is the ability to resist immediate gratification and be undeterred by the bumps on the road while moving toward what you are trying to achieve. In a survey by the American Psychological Association, the top reason given by respondents as to why they were not successful in making a change in their life was the lack of self-discipline or willpower. Twenty-seven percent of those who were surveyed reported that the lack of self-discipline was the greatest obstacle to making the life change they desired.

As for developing self-discipline, a common response to why they have not developed greater self-discipline was that their lives were too busy and that they did not have enough time to develop it. As we will explore later, this belief, along with many others, has not been supported by the research. Fortunately, what has proven to lead to the development of self-discipline is available to all of us.

Self-Discipline: A Misunderstood Power

One of the reasons why some of us may have adverse feelings toward developing self-discipline is the connotations that the term often carries with it. For many, the term "self-discipline" is associated with hard work, a lack of spontaneity, and being devoid of fun. In truth, self-discipline has less to do with the task that needs to be done and more with developing our inner potential. Further, practicing self-discipline can become both a passionate and enjoyable pursuit. This is clearly seen when learning martial arts, a musical instrument, or being a scientist or an athlete.

Every person who has achieved greatness in their field of endeavor did what they loved or what they were good at. Because they love what they do, they invest themselves heavily in it. They are great at what they do because they devote their focus to it. When doing something you love, it is easy to miss the element of self-discipline that is involved. However, developing self-discipline for doing the things that we are not passionate about is more difficult.

Research is revealing that those who are self-discipline are not necessarily better at resisting temptations than those who are not self-disciplined. Rather, they avoid putting themselves in situations that would conflict with they are trying to achieve. As a result, they less frequently find themselves having to choose between short-term pleasure and long-term regret. In other words, people who have a high level of self-control have learned how to arrange their lives in a way that makes it easier to win in the game of life.

In the following chapters, you will learn powerful strategies to gain mastery over your mind and cultivate the self-discipline that will allow you to pursue your goals and become the person you want to be.

Self-Discipline Begins in the Mind

Self-discipline is the ability to be able to control your emotions and feelings to a point where it can help you overcome your weaknesses and desire to give into temptation. People are not born with self-discipline. It is a state of mind. It is something you can learn. Once cultivated, it becomes a part of who you are. You may wonder if a change is still possible. Yes, it absolutely is.

How can self-discipline make such a difference in your life? Let's use soccer to illustrate. A team needs a goal to win. Without one, you'd be kicking the ball down the field aimlessly. Naturally, soccer players don't kick the ball aimlessly around the field to kill 90 minutes of time. They drive the ball from one direction to the next with a purpose – to score a win for their team. They are set on the goal. They push past whatever challenges come their way with determination and discipline. They do whatever it takes to make the winning kick.

Similarly, in life, if you float by day to day aimlessly with no specific goal in mind, you will not achieve anything of significance. There is no real sense of purpose. You'd just be kicking a ball around the field just to pass the time until you're done. You need to have your sights set on something specific, something strong enough that is going to give you enough mental willpower to overcome your challenges. To get your mind sufficiently focused and driven to go in the right direction, it needs a clear driving force to keep going and not stop until the finish line has been reached.

Self-Discipline and Willpower

Willpower and self-discipline are often used interchangeably, but they are not the same. Although both qualities are essential because they work together towards helping you to accomplish your goals, they have distinct differences. Willpower is the exertion when you are determined to accomplish a task. It is the level of control that an individual uses to restrain their impulses. Willpower can be short-lived and only used when the moment calls for it. Sometimes, it could be as simple as following a set of temporary rules to achieve a short-term result, like dieting or quitting smoking. In short, it is the ability to push and control yourself and your actions when needed.

Self-discipline, on the other hand, is about your mindset. It is focused on getting in touch with yourself, what you want, what you believe in and shaping your life around that belief. Self-discipline is a trait that is built for life. There is no short-term solution or rules to be followed. It is a quality that is built for a lifetime. Willpower can help you do just that.

To illustrate, think of willpower as exercise and self-discipline as muscle. With regular and consistent exercise, you can build bigger and stronger muscles. It goes without saying that a strong and healthy body brings a myriad of benefits. Similarly, with the right amount of willpower, you can develop stronger self-discipline and the benefits that come with it.

However, self-discipline, like a muscle, holds a finite supply of energy and strength. If overworked, it can get exhausted, much like how your body would feel after a vigorous full-body workout. Nobody has the ability to exercise all the time, and moments when you'll need to stop, and rest will be necessary. These kinds of lapses happen most often when we are mentally worn out or drained; after too many disappointments, perhaps, or from the strain of having to overcome challenge after challenge.

Studies on the topic have shown that large amounts of mental exertion have the potential to compromise a person's subsequent actions. You feel more discouraged when something doesn't work out quite as you hoped for, despite feeling like you've given it all your best. Your willpower will then start to diminish with each failure. Eventually, over time, it can be harder and increasingly difficult to regain willpower to make self-discipline a habit. Thus, it feels much easier to give up when things get difficult or seem impossible to accomplish.

The only way to make our bodies and muscles physically stronger is by regular exercise until it can withstand heavier pressure without fatigue. The same should be accomplished with self-discipline. It's like your "mental muscle," and it needs to get into shape. The more you work on self-discipline, the stronger and more resilient it becomes over time, until eventually, it becomes second nature to you, and the thought of giving up or quitting is not even in the picture anymore. Strengthening and fortifying this muscle provides the ultimate goal. Self-discipline is a skill you can learn.

Mental Toughness and Character

You need to be mentally tough to squash and stomp out any doubts that may creep into your mind. Mental toughness - which we'll explore further in this book - is a valuable asset when it comes to overcoming your distractions and becoming a more self-disciplined person. People who are mentally tough are not quitters. They have the drive to do what it takes to succeed; to get back up ten times after falling for nine.

A strong character is also essential for self-discipline. Often, a lack of self-discipline is a sign of weak character. Building a character will enable you to withstand any challenge you may face. If you are successful, self-discipline will never be a struggle in your life.

Be Prepared to Work Hard

Again, like a physical muscle, there is no shortcut to increased self-discipline. You have to put in the time, effort, and energy if you want to make it happen. With more discipline, you'll see more positive changes in your life. However, you'll need to make sacrifices and adjustments. There will be difficult challenges ahead, but it'll all be worth it.

The road to self-discipline is going to put you to the test and push you beyond your comfort zone. However, it will also make you a much stronger and better person. There is a reason why we often hear successful individuals attribute their success to hard work and self-discipline.

The Psychology of Self-Discipline

Special Forces Selection is designed to test the minds and bodies of potential operators. They realized a long time ago that the mind is their most important tool. This is why you too have to master your own psychology to reach your goals and take your life to the next level.

Self-Discipline is generally an act of will, so it is important to understand how the human mind works. This is done in order to convert understanding to a greater sense of self-control. Over millions of years, the human being has evolved an even more complex brain. Psychology, as a human endeavor, has shed some light into the mysteries of the mind, finally allowing us to see how things affect or motivate people and how our environment affects how we react to things that occur. In this chapter, we will look at four relevant things: the self-image, the locus of control, classical conditioning, and the psychology of motivation.

Self-Image

The way a man perceives himself affects how he reacts to the world. This is shaped by how he was raised, or the kind of people that have surrounded him. The environment he grew up in has shaped how he sees himself. There are men who have low self-esteem, and this makes them believe that they are unworthy of good things, or that they are incapable of achieving perfection.

On the other hand, there are others who have an inflated sense of self-worth, and they believe that they deserve everything without actually having to do much. These men, though they may seem powerful on the outside, are in fact hollow. Cracks on their tough shell will show overwhelming insecurity that they have spent a lifetime hiding. If a man is on the quest to becoming a true alpha male, he must be able to know the truth about himself and not give in to insecurity or the temptation to take the easy road by simply hiding under a facade.?

There can be no guarantee, however, that we will be able to understand ourselves immediately; and in fact, even psychology has not been able to get us a definite answer. But if the goal of the man is to become an alpha male, then he must be open to feedback. Negative feedback serves as a way for the man to take a detour from the path he has taken and improve himself. Focusing on negative feedback, however, won't do much good.

Negative feedback only works as a way to know if we are going the right way. However, the man must be able to discern whether or not the feedback comes from true and reliable sources--often, in the interest of politicking, people tend to lie about what they really think of you. Thus, the man must only accept feedback from the people he trusts to be brutally honest, such as a mentor or even enemies. Enemies have no interest in you and, by definition, hate you to the core. So, they will have no interest in sugar-coating anything. They will be absolute, brutally honest.

It is wise to not to be too emotional about what they have to say and instead take it as a way to improve--not for them, but for yourself, the ideal you want to achieve, or the movement you are fighting for.

Locus of Control

A man on the path to self-improvement must find out whether he blames others for the things that happen to him or if he blames himself for what happens to him. If the man blames others all the time for everything that happens to him, it can be said that his locus of control is said to be external, which means that he lets go of his power to fate or "destiny." This is the weak man's approach, especially if he believes that he is unable to change anything that happens to him. He is weak-minded and weak-willed, and he thinks that whatever happens to him is because of random chance and other people or events. This is a lazy and weak approach to life.

On the other hand, a man whose locus of control is internal tends to see everything as his fault, and if this goes to the extreme, he ends up being too overwhelmed by what is happening to him and even to the world. He might blame himself about something that happened to someone totally unrelated to him. This is unrealistic. We go back to the topic of the self-image: the man must be able to have the right information about himself in order to act upon it.

It is important that the man can balance both loci of control, and so he must be able to take responsibility for what he does. Taking responsibility strengthens the ability to take bigger risks, and it allows the man to step outside of his comfort zone. In order to become a self-disciplined alpha male, the man must be able to push himself further and further, pushing the boundaries of his comfort zone until this zone disappears.

Classical Conditioning

To challenge the idea that psychology was an armchair pseudoscience, the behaviorist movement, which included the psychologist Ivan Pavlov, brought the scientific method into the field through experimentation. Pavlov was able to show the process of training and conditioning by measuring how much dogs salivated every time a bell is rung to signify food. After the experimenter rings the bell, he puts the food out. Soon, even when he does not bring out food, the mere ringing of the bell has been shown to make the dogs react as if to get ready for food. This is called conditioning, and another way to apply this concept is reward and punishment.

People and animals tend to stay from punishment, and they tend to look for rewards. So, rewards will make us keep doing what we were doing in order to get the pleasure of that reward. Punishments work the other way around, so the balance of both reward and punishment will effectively condition a person to a certain kind of action. Because we were born with the capacity to rule ourselves, we can consciously apply this method to ourselves in order to achieve the kind of action we want to learn. Ask yourself how much pain you will get if you don't take action. For example, how much pain will you get if you don't study for your exam? Maybe you won't graduate. Now think about the short-term pain of studying versus the long-term pain of not graduating. Now think of the reward or pleasure you will get if you do the study. You will graduate with a degree and be respected by others. So in this way you can trick yourself into doing things that you don't feel like doing.

Psychology of Motivation

When people are asked who will win between a lion and a man in an arena, most people answer the lion because it is more powerful, and it has evolved to be stronger than the man. Unless that man is the mythical Hercules, the lion will no doubt devour the man. However, this does not take into consideration the sort of evolution that humanity has gone through in the past millions of years. The human has evolved a more complex brain and the ability to innovate and create weapons. Thus, a fairer fight would be between a lion and a man armed with weapons?

Humans are more complex than animals, and the difference is evident in our desire to become greater than ourselves. This book is already a testament to that. Thus, in motivating a man to become better than himself, it is important that he knows what he is fighting for. He needs a goal, and a way to know whether or not he has achieved it. Not knowing what he is fighting for, even the hardened warrior will fail. A man with a purpose is unstoppable.?

Once the man has decided on his goal, he must begin to act. Success is being and doing what you want now, and that can only be achieved if you act immediately and act as if that success is already present now. Soon, even without thinking about it, the goal will have already been reached. It is also important, then, to trust in the process or habit through the continuous application of self-discipline.

Immerse Yourself in the Culture of Self-Discipline

The first people who have introduced us to the concept of discipline were our parents. In the absence of parents, we had father and mother figures in the form of mentors, older relatives, or older peers. The way we learn about the world is through the world itself, and through the people around us. We model ourselves based on them. Discipline starts at home. You cannot help but become disciplined yourself when disciplined people surround you. A perfect example of the culture of self-discipline is the Special Operations Units.

All the men in the military follow a code. Their training, governing systems and operating procedures were all developed while considering the military code. Soldiers who show dedication in practicing this code may advance to more elite branches of the military. This separates them from other members of the armed forces and gives credit to their skills and knowledge of their craft.

When they advance to these elite branches or special forces, the types of people that they spend time with also change. Their peers in the special forces are those who are also as dedicated in their craft and in keeping their country safe.

The presence of their peers reminds the member of this branch every day of the special force's code that they live by. If everybody in the group works out regularly, it will compel the newer members to do the same. If all the members have excellent skills, the new members need to push themselves to improve their own skills. These are just some of the effects of being around people with excellent self-discipline.

Surround Yourself with Disciplined People

When developing your own self-discipline, you need to surround yourself with people who have the same goals and aspirations as you. It is even better if you can find people who are very dedicated to their work. By surrounding yourself with these types of people, you will have someone with which you can compare yourself. If you are competitive by nature, having people around you who are good at what they do can ignite your competitive spirit in you. This can be a great source of extrinsic motivation.

In your job, for example, you can look for the top performers in your office. Take the time to talk with them when they are free. If they are busy all the time, you can invite them to lunch. You can also go to the social events where the people you look up to go. If you are in the office, you can also observe them when they are working and look for what separates them from the pack.

Your goal is to spend time with them and learn about how they perform so well. It is important, also to humble yourself in the presence of more disciplined people. A child who is learning a new skill puts himself in an inferior position in order to learn faster. No self-obsessed conceited man with a superiority complex can begin to understand true self-discipline if he thinks that he is already better than everyone around him. In surrounding yourself with highly disciplined people, you must put yourself in the inferior position, like a child, in order to learn their ways and quickly become like them.

Developing Your Own Group of Highly Disciplined People

In developing all the habits discussed in this book, you will need two important components:

1. Find self-improvement buddies

Before you do any of the habits suggested in this chapter, you need to look for a person who will help you become accountable for your commitments. You need a buddy who will keep an eye on you and make sure that you do the tasks properly and on time. Ideally, you need to find a buddy who also wants to develop his own self-discipline. If you have a friend undergoing the same difficulties as you, you will have a better chance of convincing yourself to be committed to the tasks required by this book.

It is better if your buddy is ruthless in reminding you about your tasks. He should not allow you to be weak. He should be able to shout in your face when you stay in bed too long in the morning. You should do the same for him. Your standards should be high when critiquing each other's actions. You can start with a co-worker or a roommate. If you have siblings, you can also show them this book.

2. Set punishments for failure or unfinished tasks

In the military, men complete the tasks that they need to do because they do not have a choice. The drill sergeants remove the idea of having a choice. Either you do what they want, or you quit the military life because you are too weak. This prepares the soldiers for the active service. When they are in the field, they are accustomed to following orders, and they do not question the decisions decided upon by their superiors. In this kind of practice, you are able to learn the value of trusting your superiors. If you are capable of following your superiors, you will be able to set your own rules soon and follow them by yourself.

Just like in the military, the punishment that you set should be physical in nature. Push-ups and squats are the common punishments among the basic training of all the branches of the military. You could also think of undesirable chores like cleaning the backyard or the toilet and doing your buddy's laundry.

Now that you have the necessary requirements for developing special forces culture, you need to learn the habits that you need to integrate into your life. These habits are designed to make you disciplined from your waking to your sleeping hour.

The Power of Self-Discipline

Self-discipline is exactly what it says—the ability to discipline oneself. It is the ability to know what to do in situations and the fortitude to actually do what is correct in the situation. It is a habit that is vital to daily success. Truly successful people are usually highly disciplined people.

No one is born with the ability to truly self-discipline. Babies only care about being taken care of and having their needs met. As children grow, their parents are in charge of their discipline—at least in the beginning. Parents make the rules, and children follow them because small children lack the thought processes needed to make good decisions on a regular basis. Small children only see the here-and-now, the immediate gratification. They do not know and do not care that a bigger, better reward might be in store for them if they wait patiently. They lack foresight. As children grow up, they begin to see the reasoning behind their parent's rules. They begin to make choices that mirror the choices their parents have made for them in the past. They show that they are learning to discipline themselves. At this point, the parents may begin to step back a little and to loosen the reins. They may allow the child a bit more freedom in making decisions, with the understanding that the parent is available if the choice turns out to be unfavorable. In this way, the child learns in the safety of the home and with the protection of the parents to make good choices and formulate good decisions. The child learns to self-discipline.

In a perfect world, this is the way children would be raised. Unfortunately, this is the real world and not a perfect one. The problem is not that parents do not care about their children—it is that many parents do not know how to teach the art of self-discipline to their children. Maybe the parents are not self-disciplined, maybe the parents feel the child will learn it eventually, or maybe the parents simply do not want to let go complete control over the child. For whatever reason, most children are not taught self-discipline as a way of life and reach adulthood with no clue of how to be in charge of themselves.

However, the good news is that self-discipline can be learned. While best learned while growing up, as a part of learning to be an adult, it is possible to learn as an adult and begin to practice self-discipline skills immediately. Moreover, by learning self-discipline in adulthood, the person has a total buy-in to the idea. This is a personal choice. This is something that needs to be done in order to enjoy a better life. This does not mean that learning self-discipline as an adult will be easier or faster, but at least, the adult who makes the conscious choice to become more self-disciplined has a personal stake in its success.

Self-discipline is nothing more than managing one's own personal affairs. It is a way of behaving where people automatically choose to do what should be done, as opposed to what would more preferably be done. It is studying for a test instead of going to a party. It is washing dirty laundry on a regular basis, so that clean clothes are always available. It is following a budget so that future financial goals can be realized. Self-discipline is that inner voice controlling outward actions. It is using willpower to become mentally tough enough to control one's actions by oneself.

Almost anything that a person does to focus on an end goal rather than immediate satisfaction is self-discipline. The underlying problem is that it is always much easier to follow the path of impulse. Impulse is fun. Impulse is now. Impulse allows for joining the group and having a fun night on the town instead of studying and doing laundry. Impulse is the exact opposite of self-discipline.

Granted impulse is much more fun than discipline. Impulse gives the opportunity to have fun and be with friends. Impulse means staying up late and sleeping in tomorrow. Impulse means spending the extra money on the desirable frivolous toy and not saving anything this week. But impulse will not finish homework, wash clothes, follow a schedule, or save money. Self-discipline is needed for those things. Does this mean that impulse has no place in a life ruled by self-discipline? Absolutely not! Impulsive action is an almost automatic action. A cake is meant to be eaten. Self-discipline should never be so rigid that people go through life acting like little robots with no feelings and no desires. Everyone wants a cake. Having self-discipline just means eating one slice of cake and not the whole cake.

Practicing self-discipline requires great self-knowledge. Think about that for a minute. How can anything be changed if all the facts are not known? Imagine walking into a kitchen and seeing a small child and a puddle of water. The first instinct would be to believe the child spilled something. But what if someone else spilled something and then left the puddle on the floor? What if the pipe under the sink is leaking? Without knowing all the facts, there is no way to come to the correct conclusion. The path to self-discipline begins with knowing, and admitting the existence of, personal weaknesses. Everyone has those things they would rather not do. People would rather not admit to being imperfect, but all are and must be prepared to admit to imperfections to be able to begin the journey to self-discipline. The next step is to be prepared to move everyday temptations out of the way. This is usually easier said than done, but it must be done to begin along the path toward self-discipline properly. Once ready to begin, make sure to set clear, realistic goal and make a plan to achieve them. Do not be afraid to set several smaller goals as opposed to one large ultimate goal. Nothing worthwhile is ever reached in one straight path. There will be roadblocks and pitfalls along the way that will necessitate reworking the plan. So, it may be better to start with smaller goals that will give a sense of accomplishment that will help ease traveling this path.

Keep the plan simple. Self-discipline does not need to be complicated. The idea of self-discipline itself is actually a very simple concept. The plan to get to self-discipline should not be overly complicated. The plan to reach self-discipline should be as simple as possible while encompassing all aspects needed to reach the goal. A complicated plan may be impossible to achieve and will probably lead to defeat—and giving up is not an option on the road to self-discipline.

Self-discipline is a powerful tool to possess. Self-discipline is a positive force in life. It does not mean giving up those things that make life satisfying; but rather using innate strength and creativity to achieve desired goals. With self-discipline, life is more enjoyable, and the little cheats that help make life enjoyable when people have the self-discipline to learn to enjoy these little cheats only occasionally. Again, it is not necessary to completely give up cake; just do not eat the whole thing!

Self-disciplined people do not deprive themselves, but they use focus to stay on track when goals conflict with one another. Let us imagine that friends want to have fun tonight with a pub crawl. Let us also imagine there is a huge chemistry test tomorrow. The self-disciplined person would stay home and study chemistry, thus giving better odds to getting a good grade and not worrying about the risk of oversleeping and missing the test altogether. The bars will still be there another time.

People who have a high level of self-discipline are more satisfied with themselves and how their life is going. Self-discipline allows for a better sense of self and a higher level of self-esteem. Life is not out of control. Life has meaning beyond today. Worthwhile goals are in sight in the future—and this works in a cycle. Creating goals and making a plan to achieve them leads to a higher sense of self-control. A higher sense of self-control leads to more goal setting and plan making. The cycle just keeps going around.

Self-discipline allows for more time being able to do the things that will bring satisfaction and less of the things that provide no growth or satisfaction. Self-disciplined people set a goal and work toward it. Self-disciplined people are proactive, not reactive. This means they anticipate problems and work to prevent them, rather than trying to solve a problem when it occurs. Proactive people spend time every day wondering 'what if?'. What if the car does not start tomorrow? What if the washing machine breaks down? What if the tree in the backyard falls into the house? Proactive people imagine scenarios and decide on a plan of action before it is needed. If the plan is never needed, then at least there is a plan in place. Reactive people, on the other hand, spend a lot of time doing things that are not producing a future goal. Reactive people react when the problem occurs. They have no preset plan in place. If the car does not start one morning, then they scramble to find an alternate means of transportation for the day. The proactive person might give up eating lunch out every day in favor of brown-bagging lunch then saving that money for a down payment on a house. That is self-discipline. The reactive person will suddenly start scrambling trying to dig up down payment money for a house when the monthly rent increases yet again.

While missing restaurant lunches in order to save money for that future house might seem negative at the moment, it is positive in the long run. With a bit of sacrificing a future goal is achieved. Focusing on daily choices makes living more in the moment than looking toward the future. So, while planning a daily brown-bag lunch might seem like an in-the-moment choice, it is really a part of a long-term goal. Deciding on a different restaurant each day is truly in the moment—and when the goal is achieved, a tremendous sense of satisfaction replaces any feelings of deprivation that may have been lingering.

Boundaries are not scary things, but rather necessary limits to achieving a future goal. Boundaries are needed to achieve the level of self-control needed to become fully self-disciplined. Setting boundaries require knowing exactly what the future goals are and how to follow a path to achieve them. This allows the self-disciplined person to understand themselves better than most people, to be much more comfortable in their own skin than most people. This also allows the self-disciplined person to know exactly what lengths they are capable of achieving in order to reach a goal.

Moreover, becoming self-disciplined will showcase who is a friend and who is not. True friends will assist in achieving goals. True friends will not try to block the hard work needed to become self-disciplined. By making the conscious decision to become self-disciplined, the sad truth of reality means that not everyone can stay around. But the self-disciplined person has the power to create the world as they want it to be.

Self-discipline takes an extreme amount of energy to achieve. It is not just choosing to be self-disciplined—it must be constantly worked at, and that takes energy. This will require good lifestyle practices. Eat healthily, sleep regularly, exercise when possible—all these activities will energize the body and mind and make working toward the goal of self-discipline more easily attainable.

Building Mental Toughness

You have probably wondered what makes people great at what they do. Why are there great athletes, leaders, students, artists, and so on? What separates greatness from mediocrity? What do they have that others don't? Some might say these people are more talented or more intelligent, that's why they are able to achieve their goals consistently, but the truth is, intelligence or talent is not the only answer. In fact, according to studies, intelligence or talent only accounts for 30% of a person's brain. It takes a lot more than that.

So, what makes these people successful? The answer is mental toughness, or what others call grit. And what's great about it is that it can be learned. It is not something that you are born with, like intelligence or talent. So why is it important in achieving success? Let's discuss it a little bit more.

The Mental Toughness of Athletes

Athletes are known not only for their physical strength but also for their mental toughness. For instance, professional athletes have to undergo a number of tests and initiations to know how far they can go physically and mentally. And you probably think that the people who succeed in these brutal tests are the quickest, strongest, and most intelligent. Being quick, strong and intelligent sure does help a lot but what's even more useful is the person's perseverance, resilience, and passion in what he or she does.

You may be strong and intelligent, but if your mind already gives up, then there is really nothing you can do about it. Your mental strength is the trait that will push you to the finish line, not intelligence or strength, especially if it is a long and arduous test.

This is what most athletes have in common—they have the mental toughness that allows them to endure any physical, emotional, and mental hardships that they had to undergo to be able to become worthy competitors in their chosen sport.

Who Exhibits Mental Toughness?

Aside from athletes, other groups of people also show mental toughness. These are people who excel at what they do. For example, it may be difficult to get into an Ivy League school but getting in is a lot easier than staying. This is because you need mental toughness or grit to be able to maintain a high GPA while inside the school.

People who join contests such as the National Spelling Bee contests are not necessarily the most intelligent students in their class. They are most often the ones who show grit and who are committed to spending hours to study new words and practice a couple of hours every day. You may be a talented writer but to be able to become a successful writer, you have to spend several hours a day not only writing but also reading books, which takes mental toughness.

Successful athletes have to undergo intensive training and practice. Kobe Bryant, Cristiano Ronaldo, and Roger Federer didn't get to where they are right now solely because of talent. Actors and actresses who are excellent at their craft also have a lot of grit in them. They have to study their characters deeply, memorize scripts, and go to shooting schedules at the wee hours of the day.

Regular people employees also show mental toughness on a daily basis. These are the employees who finish their tasks on or before the set deadline. They are also highly reliable because their bosses know that they will not slack off.

Look around you every day, and you will see people showing mental toughness. You probably even had exhibited mental toughness before when you forced yourself to finish something that you have to do even when temptations surround you. You didn't give in, and you didn't give up no matter what until you achieved what you have to do. It is accepting discomfort for the sake of reaching your goal. That's mental toughness for you.

Daily Practices for Mental Toughness

Like the athletes, you also need to experience discomfort that will improve your mental toughness. There are practices that you can incorporate in your daily routine that will help improve your mental toughness and will, in turn, develop your self-discipline. Here are some of them.

1. Take cold showers

Did you know that the Spartans bathe in ice-cold water on a daily basis because "comfort zone" is not a part of their vocabulary? In fact, this is a technique also done by world-class athletes because of how effective it is in improving their mental toughness. They take a cold shower for as long as 30 minutes! You might think this is unnecessary suffering, but it is not because taking cold showers has a lot of benefits such as boosting your immune system, increasing levels of testosterone, reducing inflammation, and so on. When the cold water touches your skin for the first time, try not to yell or wince. Just bear it and keep your mind and body as relaxed as possible by taking deep breaths. Try to stay in the cold water for at least 30 seconds and just make it longer as you get used to the coldness.

2.Minimize social media usage

What do you need social media for, anyway, aside from sharing memes and other unimportant stuff? Moreover, you just sometimes get negative feelings such as envy, irritation, insecurity, and so on when you log in to your numerous social media accounts. People become addicted to it because it is like crack. It gives you that unnatural high with every like, comment, and notification that you get. When you scroll through your newsfeed, you will most likely click on a post that catches your attention, you will read it, and before you know it, you are on your tenth post and reading comments of people you don't really know about something that you don't really care about. It's a waste of time.

It takes a lot of mental toughness to unplug from social media. You can either stop using it completely or try to use it only when necessary, like for communication or sharing important stuff. But minimize social media usage as much as you can and just spend your free time doing more productive things. Believe it or not, Steve Jobs didn't let his kids use iPads because he knows how toxic it can get once people start to go online and use social media.

3. Get out of bed right away

When you hear your alarm go off in the morning, do not press snooze and do not stay in your bed even for just one minute longer. Jump out of bed when you wake up in the morning and do not tell yourself "ten more minutes" or "I'll just rest my eyes" because let's not fool ourselves here. People who say these things and do them usually end up getting up a lot later than their intended time. Get out of bed right away and do something to keep your blood flowing. Splash your face with cold water, make coffee or tea, prepare breakfast, and just do anything to wake yourself up. This is all just mind over matter. And you will feel a lot better later on when you realize how much you were able to finish in a day because you woke up early.

4. Sleep on the floor

You can also try sleeping on the floor once in a while. You don't necessarily need to give up your comfortable bed for good. Just do this from time to time to help you build your mental toughness. For a really tough challenge, sleep without a blanket. Use a thin sheet if you are not ready for the difficulty level. Do you think the Spartans and Special Forces slept on a soft bed with fluffy pillows and a warm blanket? If they did, they'd probably still wake up really early for their drills. But they sure didn't have this luxury. So, if you want to be just like them, try to experience this once in a while. Believe me, this will make you appreciate your bed and pillows and blanket a lot more than you used to.

5. Do small exercises

This will not be your regular full-blown workout. That is another thing that you should be doing even if you are not trying to lose weight because it will keep your body strong and healthy. These mini workouts are those workouts that you can incorporate in your everyday life. This is especially helpful if you work in a 9 to 5 job sitting in front of the computer the whole day. Try to do a set of 25 to 50 squats, sit-ups, push-ups, jumping jacks, or any other form of exercise that you can do in your office. Try to do this at least every hour or depending on how much your office will allow you to take a break during office hours. Instead of going for a cigarette break or to the pantry to have snacks, get out of your comfort zone and instead do some exercises that will keep you from being completely sedentary.

6. Move slowly

You might think that this tip is counterintuitive because slowness is often not associated with success and achieving goals. But this does not literally mean working at a slower pace. It just means that you do not make impulsive actions and snap decisions. For example, when you go to your car, open the door, and sit in the driver's seat, what's the first thing you do? You probably connect your phone to the car stereo to play some of your favorite songs. Why not consider doing it deliberately by not rushing? It is mindful of every move and decision you make. If you are no impulsive and you are deliberate at everything you do, you will keep yourself from making mistakes and wrong decisions. By moving in a more deliberate style, you are teaching yourself to be more in control of your actions. You will take more time to react to thoughts and emotions and also to make important decisions.

7. Get dirty

Some people are so afraid to get themselves dirty because getting dirty is way out of their comfort zone. Although being clean is something that we should all strive for, there is nothing wrong with getting yourself dirty from time to time. NOTE: If you are already a slob, then you should skip this tip or consider doing the reverse—get yourself cleaned up. Try to walk inside your house or in your front yard with bare feet. If a piece of food like a chip or cookie falls on the floor, do not be afraid to pick it up and eat it. Squish bugs such as mosquitoes using your bare hands. Try not to take a shower at least once a week (unless you have just been working out and you were sweating heavily). Just basically try not to be comfortably clean from time to time. Did you know that the Spartans and Special Operations Unit sometimes go for days without showering especially when they are in the middle of combat? Try to do this yourself and see how much your mental toughness will improve.

8. Read

Reading a book can make you tougher mentally because it helps you improve your mental focus for a long period of time. Read a book for a couple of hours every day that can teach you a thing or two about delayed gratification, unlike the television and online videos that are considered passive entertainment and do not really contribute anything to improving your mental toughness. Reading is also an activity that allows you to use your mind active and learning new words and information is always a welcome bonus.

Four mental toughness techniques inspired by war

War is never a good thing, but you have to do what you have to do, so just make the most of the situation by finding the silver lining in the satiation, such as learning some life lessons from it. You already know by now that the epitome of mental toughness is the Special Operations Units or the Spartans. Both are, without a doubt, mentally tough. And they have to be mentally tough, apart from also being physically and emotionally strong, in preparation for war. So, what mental toughness techniques inspired by a war that you can try in your day-to-day life? Check out the following.

1. Train to increase confidence

The training of the Spartans and the Special Forces are repetitive— they have to do things over and over again until they master the task. And isn't this how practice and training works? You repeatedly do things until you become good at it. And when you are good at something, it gives you a boost of confidence.

The number one goal of the Special Forces is to achieve the mission, whatever it is. The protection of the members of the troop only comes in second. It is safe to say that completing the mission is more important than the safety of the soldiers. Leaders and commanders have no other choice but to send their team into combat for them to achieve the goal. It is a must in any war. And as a leader, you have to show confidence in your decision to send out troops who could get killed while doing their duty. Whether you are leading five or five hundred people, you need to project 100% confidence because they also get their confidence from their leaders.

Aggressive training for confidence for the soldiers also applies to ordinary people who want to improve their mental toughness. What you can do is to start practicing steadily and deliberately. Try to overcome small obstacles first to slowly gain confidence before you tackle bigger challenges in your life.

As an exercise, think of something that you badly want to do, but you do not know how to do it well, for instance, playing the guitar. Consider it as your little petri dish, or experiment. Do some exercises or activities every day that will make you improve your guitar-playing skills, such as playing short and simple pieces then later on moving to more difficult ones. You will gain confidence as you learn the skill over time that will give you mental toughness to endure anything that will keep you from reaching your goals.

2. Develop your sense of duty

Sometimes, it is more effective to simply tell yourself that "it's your job" for you to finish what you need to do. It is the simplest and easiest form of mental toughness. Soldiers train and practice because they know that it is their job. Their job is to fight for their country and protect their countrymen against the enemies. And also, they also benefit personally, such as earning a monthly salary or in the case of the Spartans, becoming a citizen. If you understand your responsibilities and you know the consequences of not doing them, it will be much easier to finish tasks.

As an exercise, write down all your responsibilities for the different roles you play in life—employee, parent, partner, etc. Tape your list somewhere you can easily see and tweak them every week. Your responsibilities are your duties—duties to your employers, to your loved ones, and also to yourself. It may not be a matter of life and death, but a lot of people still depend on you. And it is a man's duty to finish what he has started and to do the things that he had agreed to do because a man keeps his word.

3. Do it for your troop

The idea behind the military will not work if the members do not have teamwork. In fact, they train soldiers to remove any sense of individualism when inside the barracks and when they do their job. This is because someone who is too individualistic may end up not following orders of the commander and can be disastrous in any operation. People who care more about themselves than about the team will also save their behind's first than look after their team members, something that is highly discouraged in the military. In fact, the Marines has a saying that "No one gets left behind," whether that soldier is alive or already died or is beyond help. Everyone has to be saved.

The point here is that it is important to have a strong group of people around you who will support you no matter what and vice versa. You do not need to die for them. It can be something like being there for each other when one member of the family is fighting a serious illness, trying to keep your company afloat with your team, or when you just lost your job, and you need to start searching for a new one —situations like these can make or break a man. But if you have the right group of people around you, then you will surely overcome such challenges and will, therefore, increase your mental toughness.

For your exercise, make a list of all the people whom you trust, and you know you can depend on. Strengthen your relationship with these people and let go of people in your life who do nothing but let you down or make you feel worthless. You will be more likely to succeed and overcome big challenges in life if you are surrounded by these positive people.

4. Take pride in what you do

Awards and rewards for a job well done are helpful when it comes to boosting someone's morale and motivation. But what's even more important than any trophy or medal is how you feel inside. Taking pride in what you do, and your accomplishments is already a kind of reward in itself. Soldiers in combat do incredible and amazing things on a daily basis, and they do not receive special awards for them.

And this is not done intentionally by the government because they try to recognize these soldiers' achievements as much as they can. But of course, not everything is noticed and recorded, and most of these soldiers just keep their accomplishments to themselves, not wanting any form of recognition because it already gave them a feeling of pride. And for them, that's enough.

In your life, just because you do not get recognition for something that you do does not mean you have to stop doing it. Keep on doing what you need to do not to get awards but to take pride in yourself. And once you take pride in what you do, you will become mentally tougher because your resilience to endure does not only come from the outside but more importantly from the inside.

How to Apply Self-Discipline in Your Life

A common misconception of self-discipline is that it is some sort of magic wand, capable of solving problems and creating success all on its own. While self-confidence is critical in order to achieve success, it is not the be-all and end-all. In a way, it can be seen as the engine that enables a vehicle to reach its destination. Needless to say, no vehicle can move from point A to point B without an engine. However, the engine can only perform its functions when properly maintained. Without such things as fuel and oil, an engine will stop working, regardless of how well made it is. Self-discipline acts in exactly the same way. Only when you invest the necessary energy into your self-discipline will it function correctly, taking you to your desired destination. This chapter will focus on the different types of energies needed to fuel your self-discipline, showing you how to keep your engine running at peak efficiency.

Creating your motivation

One of the most important energies that your self-discipline relies on is motivation. This is probably the single thing that keeps so many people from achieving the success that they so desperately desire. No amount of self-discipline can help you to achieve your goals in life unless you have the motivation needed to keep things moving along. In short, self-discipline without motivation is no different than an engine without gas.

Before discussing various ways of creating and maintaining motivation, it is first necessary to discuss some of the pitfalls that serve to undermine and even eliminate motivation. One of the most common of these pitfalls is pursuing someone else's goal. This is usually seen in children who are studying to pursue a career that their parents have chosen for them. How many times have you seen or heard of people becoming doctors, lawyers and the like simply because it is what their parents wanted? While many achieve their goals, a good deal more falls short. The reason for this is that they lack the motivation to pursue someone else's dream. Even those who do achieve the goals usually do so without any real passion or desire, resulting in a life that is more of a dull existence than an actual vibrant and rewarding life.

Therefore, the first thing you need to do is to ensure that your goals actually belong to you and that they aren't ideas placed into your mind by someone else. Before you begin to plan and plot your way to a destination you need to decide that the destination is where you really want to go, if it isn't, you will face an uphill battle each and every step along the way. Time after time you will struggle with the obstacles and pitfalls along the way to achieving your goal, without any real incentive to persevere. Regardless of whether you are pursuing a dream to please your parents, a spouse, or even social norms, it all boils down to the same scenario. If the dream doesn't come from your heart, you won't have the fire in your belly that drives, you to your success.

Once you have determined that your goal truly belongs to you the next step is to discover the reason behind the goal. Every goal has an underlying cause, something that makes a particular goal worth pursuing. For example, you might desire to go to medical school and become a doctor. While being a doctor is a good thing there will be an underlying reason for you making that choice. More often than not that reason will be to save lives and help people who are suffering. Thus, while becoming a doctor is the goal it is not the reason, rather saving lives and helping people is the reason. This is the 'why' behind your dream, and it is a pivotal source of motivation that will fuel your self-discipline every step of the way.

Alternatively, you might want to achieve a goal because of the lifestyle you believe it will offer you. For example, the lifestyle of an Olympic athlete might be the very thing you desire more than anything else in this life. Living a life of singular purpose, constantly striving to perfect your abilities in order to compete in the most prestigious competitive event on earth could be your truest, most heartfelt dream. In this case, envisioning the gold medal being placed around your neck is the source of motivation that will enable you to overcome all 0f the setbacks, pitfalls, and struggles you face along the way. No matter what your motivation is, the important thing is to discover it so that it can help fuel the self-discipline you need in order to achieve your dream.

Reward and punishment

Another way to establish motivation in your life is to create a system of reward and punishment. This might seem a bit harsh at first, especially the punishment part; however, it's not as bad as it sounds. The idea of punishment for failure shouldn't be interpreted as causing yourself pain and suffering whenever you fall short, rather it is a matter of withholding certain pleasures from yourself when you engage in negative behavior. By withholding things that bring pleasure when you engage in negative behavior and indulging in them when you put forth your best efforts you will create a very real value system in your mind that will redefine how you see self-discipline.

One of the reasons why so many people never pursue a dream or a meaningful goal is that they have an easy enough life without achieving their dreams. People can indulge in their favorite coffee drinks, fancy pastries or any other number of tasty temptations any time, any day. This turns those things that would be rewards into everyday items, removing their true value as well as the potential they have for helping you to succeed. By withholding such things from yourself when you go astray, you create a sense of punishment that you will want to avoid. Again, this isn't about creating pain in your life; rather it is about encouraging you to steer clear of certain behaviors or activities.

A good example of this is if you wind up procrastinating on a project. By allowing yourself to avoid starting a project you undermine your chances of success. This is certainly a behavior that you want to eliminate from your life as quickly as possible. The best way to do this is to train your mind to see procrastination as something undesirable. If you refrain from eating ice cream, if you love ice cream, every time you procrastinate you send yourself a clear message. No action equals no ice cream. At first this may seem a bit extreme; however, your mind requires encouragement, both positive and negative. Eventually, procrastination won't hold the same power over you as it once did. Instead, your mind will resist any urges to be lazy so that you can enjoy those things that bring you happiness at the end of the day.

In order to make this an effective tool it is important to define failure clearly. This isn't a failure in terms of when things don't work out according to plan. Rather, this is a failure in terms of self-discipline. Being lazy, doing a half-hearted job, blaming others for your own mistakes and other similarly negative behaviors are the things you want to eliminate from your day to day life. Therefore, they are the things you want to define as failures in your mind. Whenever you give in to these negative behaviors, you have to take responsibility and punish yourself in a way that makes those behaviors less and less desirable.

The other side of this is rewarding yourself for good behavior. This is the same practice, only in reverse. Rather than depriving yourself of your favorite things for bad performance you indulge in your favorite things on days that you do well. After a while, your mind will identify hard work, honesty, integrity and all of the positive actions that embody self-discipline with the pleasure that comes from rewarding yourself at the end of the day. This will encourage you to pursue those actions that will take you closer and closer to success each and every day. It all comes down to a matter of accountability and commitment. By holding yourself accountable for your actions, you will establish better habits that will lead to better results. By committing to this, you will develop a sense of self-discipline that will enable you to redefine any action or effort in a way that makes it as desirable as the result you are striving to achieve.

Creating a competitive environment

Finally, there is the aspect of creating a competitive environment. What most people don't realize is that the energy in their mind is directly affected by the energy of their surroundings. Thus, the more time a person spends in a negative environment, the more negative their energies will become. The very same thing holds true in terms of people. When a person surrounds themselves with negative people, their mindset will become negative as a result. The solution is to create a competitive environment. This is what is meant by placing yourself in the right places and around the right people in order to bring out your best in terms of effort, talent, and overall self-discipline.

The first step to creating a competitive environment is to distinguish the difference between positive and negative environments clearly. Any place that encourages laziness, self-pity, negative thinking and other such toxic energies is a place that you need to avoid. The last thing you need to do is to put yourself in an environment that will encourage the behaviors you are trying to rid yourself of. Such environments can include cheap bars where people go to drown their sorrows in alcohol and thus avoid facing their problems head-on. Basically, any place that attracts deadbeats, dropouts and those with low self-esteem are places you want to steer well clear of.

This approach can be applied to people as well. One of the biggest problems that most people face is that they aren't careful with regard to the people they spend time with. Subsequently, the average person spends as much time around negative people each and every day as they do around positive people. In fact, they probably spend more time with negative people as there are usually more of those to be found. The result is that their self-esteem, outlook on life and even their hopes and dreams can become tainted by the negative energy of the people around them. The more time you spend around spiteful people with little or no ambition is the more likely you will become like them. Therefore, in order to protect your self-discipline, it is essential that you avoid negative people as much as possible.

In addition to avoiding negative places and people, it is critical that you find positive places and people to replace them with. Just as the negative energy from spiteful, lazy people can influence your own energy, so too can the positive energy from successful, highly motivated people. In a way, it's a bit like the old axiom "you are what you eat." When you eat junk food, your health suffers. Alternatively, when you eat healthy food your physical and mental wellbeing increases. The exact same thing occurs with regard to mental energy. Therefore, it is vital that you surround yourself with energetic, positive people who encourage you to be your best in order to increase your own sense of motivation and self-worth.

Finding places of positive energy will go a long way to keeping you motivated as well. Such places can differ, depending on the person, so the important thing is to discover what works best for you. Most of the time you will want to choose a place that reflects the particular dream or goal you are pursuing at the moment. If you are studying to become a doctor, for example, you might want to spend time in a hospital where you can watch successful doctors help people the way you want to. This will help you to keep your eyes on the proverbial prize, which will increase your energies exponentially. If you are trying to start a business, you can go to any successful business or store and soak in the feeling of success that permeates such a place. The important thing is that you find an environment that helps you to stay focused not only on your goals and dreams but also on the fact that you have what it takes to achieve those goals and dreams. This will help you to keep your head up even when things aren't going your way. Always remember that the successful people you are hoping to emulate suffered the same setbacks and failures as you, yet they made it to the end, as will you if you maintain your sense of self-discipline.

Consistency and How to Develop Positive Habits

It is our habits that define us. Our results will directly reflect our level of effort and quality of results. Positive habits are habits that empower us and are aligned with our goals, while negative habits prevent us from having the happiness and success we desire. Habits can be developed at an early age or even learned from our peers. It is also possible to deliberately create new habits that would bring cumulative effects over a period and transform one's life. Most people do not know that it can take around 28 days to create a habit, and most have habits that were developed unknowingly.

Cultivating good habits is a very effective way of becoming self-disciplined. This is because most of what we do and how we behave daily are determined by our habits. Therefore, having the right habits will go a long way in bringing discipline into our lives.

However, it can be hard to form a new habit or change when a habit has been developed over a long period of time because there are neural pathways that are etched in the brains. These neural pathways serve the purpose of connecting neural networks to effortlessly carry out a particular function such as walking, abusing drugs, or drinking water without having to think. We tend to have some bad habits that have a negative effect on our lives because over a long time the neural pathways become a part of us, and it becomes very hard to shake off the bad habits and develop good ones. But, if you can make a conscious decision to develop good habits in your life, you'll find that becoming disciplined will be easier. It is not an overnight process, and it takes time to form new habits.

You should evaluate and find out the activities that have the potential to transform your life for the better if you commit to doing them every day for a period of 30 days.

Define the things that are most important to you, when you wake up each the morning, identify them and be determined that they must be accomplished that day. Dedicate time to do them, every single day for the next month. If your goal is to become productive at work, show up early every day, refuse to browse social media while on duty, and create time to do this only during leisure after work. If your goal is to get into shape, spend a definite amount of time in the gym every day. No matter what your goal is—do something towards achieving it daily.

Know that every day matters. Set out to accomplish any goal, or task that you have set for yourself because this will determine whether your dream will become a reality or not. The key to self-discipline is consistent with your good habits.

Get Started Even When You Do Not Feel Like It

If you make excuses, you will not be able to develop discipline nor achieve your goals. Naturally, it is easier to want to do a thing when we know that it is entertaining and pleasurable but disciplining yourself requires that you carry out important tasks even when they appear intimidating and/or boring. If you must wait till when you feel is the right time before you do something you will not achieve much in your life. Waiting for a feel-good moment before studying for exams or hitting the gym is the perfect recipe for failure.

Successful people become who they are because through sheer willpower and determination, they rose above their weaknesses, developed good qualities and habits. You must be ready to have a greater mastery of your personality and exhibit the strength to overcome all obstacles including yourself until you succeed. Ability to do the right things even when you don't feel like it is the means to self-confidence and achieving greatness.

Force Yourself Until it Becomes Routine

Sometimes we have to force ourselves to do the things that will benefit us. It can be hard to stay disciplined on the days when the motivation to do something is low. We need to push ourselves and just get started. In order to convince yourself to do things when you don't feel like, you can use the 5- minute rule. It is important to be aware of our flaws and strength and use them to our advantage. One of the mind's greatest weaknesses is that it can be a struggle to get things started, but once we summon the courage and get started, it becomes easier to continue.

If you are feeling reluctant to start working on something important, convince yourself that you will do it for only 5 minutes, it could be performing aerobic exercises, replying to emails or meditating for a short period. Once you start you will discover that the activity will continue for more than the 5 minutes than your mind is conditioned to do, this is because you have overcome the initial barrier of personal resistance and will get into a state of flow.

Set Reminders

Maintaining focus can be hard, therefore, to remain on task, ensure that your goals are not far away from your mind and attention. Remind yourself about your goals regularly b using journals, diaries, and reminders to stay on top of your daily activities. For example, if you are to go on an early morning run set the alarm for the time you have to wake up; you can set a reminder ahead of time to notify you when it is close to the time to meditate. Use your smartphone as a tool to become more productive by setting reminders, alarms on the tasks and activities you need to carry out. You are what you repeatedly do; therefore, the process of becoming successful does not happen just by action but by good habits.

Continuous Personal Improvement

To become the best you can be, you must consistently improve your knowledge. Dedicate efforts to investing in yourself by expanding your knowledge and skills.

A way of doing this is to read daily, up to an hour if you can. Having knowledge about your goals can be very helpful, for instance by reading relevant articles and newsletters, you can easily learn about a variety of diets to live by if your goal is to eat healthily and stay fit.

Listen to relevant audiotapes, podcasts that can keep you updated about the happenings and knowledge related to your career or field of interest. Endeavor to learn something new every day, make it a habit. You should also attend meetups and seminars to constantly increase your knowledge and equip you better to achieve your goals.

Persistence Is the Key to Self-Discipline

The desire for a more self-disciplined personality will not be enough unless you persist and are willing to keep that momentum going. Persistence is another important trait you'll need to build a strong character. Your very success will depend on your ability to persist even when the odds are not in your favor. Setbacks will happen, wrenches will be thrown in your plan. You must persist in the face of them all. That is the epitome of what self-discipline is all about.

Self-Discipline and Self-Esteem Are Best Friends

Self-discipline and self-esteem are two interconnected traits. Self-esteem is part of that equation and is also heavily affected by fear.

Every time you let fear conquer you, your self-esteem will be among those that suffer. However, the opposite is true as well. When you use self-discipline and persistence, despite any hesitance on your part, to accomplish what needed to be done, your self-esteem will get a much-needed boost. You'll also have more self-confidence.

Every achievement that you make with self-discipline will enhance your self-esteem more, and fuel the desire to keep going, going and going. Before you know it, you're on a roll, and you have become an unstoppable force.

Persistence can be a surprisingly rewarding quality. When you power through a task (along with willpower), the result is going to make you feel much happier and better about yourself. As part of this ripple effect, those feelings will drive you to want to do more, to see just how far you can go if you only persist on a task. Even if you were to have bucket loads of self-discipline, if you do not persist, the success that may be within your grasp may end up sliding further out of reach.

Why is persistence such an important quality to possess as you become a more self-disciplined person? Here's why:

•	Persistence is among the first signs that you are transforming into a more ambitious person. Setting all the goals and actions plans in the world is not going to be enough if you are going to give up and not persevere each time you are knocked on your bottom. If you want to become a successful person, ambition and drive are going to be the levers which are going to help drive you to the top.

•	It makes victories that much more valuable. If success always came easy, we would never learn to appreciate it. Being a persistent person will allow let you appreciate every accomplish and make every victory taste just a little bit sweeter because you know you poured your heart, soul, blood, sweat, and tears into making it happen.

•	It is good for character building because persistence is living proof that you have it within you to achieve a goal. Each time you push through a difficult period, you will emerge that much stronger and better.

•	It will fine tune you regarding your weaknesses and fears. Part of achieving success is to be able to identify them. When you persist through one weakness and overcome it, you will automatically start looking for the next weakness that you can work through.

Persistence as a Part of Your Character

Being ready for success in life will partly be dependent on your response to setbacks. Setbacks have a way of frustrating our emotions with feelings of despondency and discouragement. We end up confused as to why it has happened in spite of all the effort you've put in. These seemingly small failures may even push us to give in.

Setbacks give you the perfect opportunity to rise to the challenge, to pull in persistence and self-discipline together. You'll remember that what matters is not how hard or how many times you fall. It's your ability to get back up and dust yourself off that really counts. Shake off the frustration. Build yourself and believe that you can overcome this trial. Keep the following key points in mind:

Key #1 Be Optimistic

Having an optimistic outlook is the first and most important key to developing persistence. It's the unwavering belief that no matter what happens, things will work out in the end. You can develop optimism by building and also improving your self-belief and self-confidence. Persistent and disciplined people do not just sit idly, feeling sorry for themselves whenever challenges arise.

Look to your role models and your mentors. They would not be where they are today if they had allowed setbacks and difficulties to stop them and the challenges have surely been many. Yet, they remain optimistic.

Key #2 No Room for Excuses

Pointing fingers and blaming the hand you've been dealt with is not a winning attitude. Unaccountability will only feed into that negativity cycle of feeling sorry for yourself. The result is often diminished willpower and, eventually, giving in to a seemingly difficult task.

Key #3 Focus on the Solution

The key to winning at persistence is to focus on the solution, not the problem. You have to realize that setbacks, however difficult, are ultimately temporary. Thus, always have the solution as a priority.

Every time you face an unexpected setback, train your mind in such a way that its first impulse is to think and focus on resolving the current issue. Staying focused on a solution will give you the determination to persist and keep going until the setback is resolved. Use self-discipline as a springboard for that persistence so that nothing deters you.

Key #4 Identify Problem Areas

It's important that you find the areas in your life where persistence will be most helpful. These areas will most likely be where fear is holding you back. Identify specific areas and write them down so you can better reflect on them. Ask yourself why persistence has lacked in this area before. What can you do differently this time? Create an action plan that is detailed and precise.

Once you've determined the areas in your life where persistence is needed, you'll need to go back to Key # 3: find a solution, or solutions, and focus your persistence and willpower on what you've found. With self-discipline, you can also prove victorious over these problem areas and thereby strengthen your persistence.

Key #5 Think of Setbacks as Gifts

Considering a setback as a gift instead of a curse may be the last thing on your mind. However, this method actually works. If you think about the past challenges and setbacks that you faced which you managed to overcome eventually anyway, instead of looking at the downside, consider the takeaway lessons each setback left you with. Did it make you a much stronger person? Did it turn out to be a blessing in disguise? Did it add something of value to your life in a way you might not otherwise have had the opportunity of experiencing? If you can train yourself to view each setback as a gift instead of a demotivating element, you will do wonders to transform your persistence and levels of self-discipline.

Self-Discipline and Happiness

Happiness- It can come freely without any form of struggle. Nobody is always happy, but some are definitely more satisfied than others. Research reveals that achieving happiness has little to do with material goods or large businesses; it all comes down to the approach to life and the quality of your relationships.

Try to be optimistic- In the 1970s, researchers followed people who had won the lottery, finding that a year later, they were no happier than people who won the lottery. This phenomenon is called "Hedonistic Adaptation," and suggests that each of us has a 'basic level' of happiness. Regardless of what happens, whether good or bad, the effect on our happiness is temporary, once "finished" the human being tends to return to the basic level. Some people have a higher level than others, and this is partly due to genetic conformations but is influenced above all, by the way, you "think." So, while this article will help you boost your happiness, the mere fact of improving your attitude towards life will improve it permanently.

Try always to have something to do- It is essential to get up every morning with the awareness of working towards achieving a goal. Having something to do makes you see the "big scheme of things," and you will not feel like you're working mechanically, without actually finishing anything. Do something for someone else; when you do something significant, discover that inspiration comes naturally.

Follow your instinct- During an experiment, two groups of people were asked to choose a poster to take home. The first group should have done this by analyzing their motivation, for and against, while the second group was suggested to follow their instincts. The result —two weeks later, the group that decided without overthinking was more pleased with their posters than those who instead have chosen the choice carefully. Now, some of our decisions are more important than selecting a poster, but once the decision has been carefully evaluated, the options to be weighed are probably very similar, and the difference will only affect your happiness temporarily. So, the next time you have a decision to make, and you only have two or three options left, choose the one you feel is right and let yourself go. Never repent of your decisions anyway. Live according to the 3 C rule of life: Choices, Chances, Changes (Choices, Opportunities, Changes). It is necessary to decide to have an opportunity, or your life will never change.

Earn money enough to cover your basic needs- Food, a roof and clothing. In the United States, for example, the magic number is $ 40,000 a year. Any amount beyond that does not necessarily mean being happier. Remember the lottery winners we talked about before? Once you can earn enough to support your basic needs, your happiness will not be affected by how much money you have, but by your level of optimism. Your ease could increase with your salary, but that's not what influences people's happiness. It seems to be one of the biggest causes of boredom. That's why it's important to push yourself beyond your comfort zone to continue to grow inwardly.

Surround yourself with friends and family- or move where they live so that you can see them more often. We live in a society in constant motion, in which people pursue work around the continent and sometimes even around the world. We do it because we think that the increase in wages makes us happier when, in fact, our relationship with family and friends has a much greater impact on our happiness. So, the next time you think about a transfer, you think you need an increase of over $ 100,000 to make up for the loss of happiness you would have by leaving relatives and friends. In any case, if relationships with family and friends are not really the best, or even non-existent, and you tend to move elsewhere, choose a location where you will earn the same amount of money as everyone else; according to research, people feel safer financially (and happier) when they live in a context with similar economic bases, regardless of the specific amount of money involved.

Try always to have deep, meaningful conversations- Research carried out by an Arizona University psychologist showed how investing more time by participating in meaningful and profound conversations, instead of simple chats, can improve the perception of happiness.

Find happiness in the work you do currently- With a positive attitude, you will always succeed in getting the best out of any job, and if you have good social relationships, your sense of gratification will be independent of the work you do. You will find satisfaction in daily interactions with the people you care about. This doesn't mean that you should not aspire to a better job to be happier, but only to say that you should understand that the possible influence on your happiness is much less than your mentality and the relationship with people close to you.

Smile- Science suggests that smiling, regardless of whether you are happy or not, improves your mood. So, do it every time you can! In addition, having enough money to pay for your expenses allows you to focus your energy on more productive aspects of life, such as pursuing happiness rather than always being on the "defensive."

Forgive- Research conducted by university students has shown that having a more permissive attitude contributes to improving the functioning of the cardiovascular system. One can practically say that forgiving is good for the heart—literally. Although not yet known as having a direct influence on the heart, the study seems to suggest that it may actually lower the level of perception of stress.

Make friends- In a 2010 study published by Harvard researchers in the American Sociological Review, people who regularly went to church reported greater satisfaction with their lives than those who did not. The critical factor was the quality of church friendships. The "goers" who did not have close friendships were no happier than "non-visitors." When the researchers compared the two groups with the same number of "friendships," they noticed that people whose friendships were born in the church had a more satisfying life. We have therefore thought about how to create a friendship based on sharing a common interest and belief (and consistently meet based on that) make the difference, therefore, if the church does not fit your interests, consider finding another thing to be passionate about and forge relationships with people with whom to connect regularly based on that. Furthermore, interacting with other people who share your interest will make you feel happier thanks to the feeling of gratification and well-being that comes with it. This is because during these interactions endorphin and dopamine are released - neurotransmitters responsible for the sense of happiness and relaxation. In other words, our body is designed to make us feel happier when we are involved in social interactions.

The fact that others seem happy does not necessarily mean that they really are. People might pretend, especially if they are too involved in things on paper that give happiness as a foregone conclusion; it's really hard to admit "having put eggs in the wrong basket." Do not be afraid to admit you're down and need a push to get up. On the contrary, if a person has a negative influence on you, do not be afraid to remove it from your life. It is also important to keep in close contact with relatives and a small circle of good friends. Nurture love and support.

When it seems like you cannot achieve happiness despite all the efforts you are doing to get it, do something crazy. Stupid, crazy, strange actions may seem to make no sense, but they could raise your morale - just for the pleasure of doing it. Furthermore, try to understand the fundamental concept that happiness is a state of mind and not something that can be defined objectively. It is possible to change this mental state in many ways, including:

• Turn up the volume of your favorite music and dance stupidly. Talk to yourself, looking in the mirror.

• Taste new food.

• Unusually reorganize your room.

• Write a quote on your mirror/wall/ cabinet—it can be a funny phrase or something that inspires you always to give the best.

• Shout as loud as you can (warn your family members first) and jump around.

• If it's a beautiful sunny day, wear your costume, go out in the garden and get wet with a pump.

• If you have children, how much you love them and how proud you are of them, and that you would do anything to help them.

• Listen only to cheerful music, which you cheer up.

• Surround yourself with colors that will put you in a good mood. Change that dark wallpaper with colors like blue or yellow.

- If you are not happy, remember that it is not necessary to have a huge house and be rich; the important thing is to live in serenity and have the freedom to do whatever you want.

- Nobody's perfect! Do not be discouraged by ONE thing that does not go as planned.

- Always wait for the best. You might think it's better to expect the worst, so you'll never be disappointed. But in the long run, it will be better always to expect the best as you can always be proud of it, regardless of what may happen.

If you are constantly dissatisfied or depressed, it would be good to seek professional help. Happy people are not always happy. Everyone has his moments of sadness, frustration, guilt, anger and so on. The happy people are simply more likely to have a mental state set on the most optimistic thoughts. We all feel bad in the darkest moments of our life but try to overcome them and live in the moment, trying to be happy in everything you do.

Self-Discipline and Living in the Moment

Living in the present is often not easy. Oftentimes, our mind is filled with thoughts of past regrets and anxieties about future events, and as a result, we struggle to enjoy the present. If you have difficulty living in the moment, you can find support in some simple strategies. Face your days by making small gestures that help you stay in the present, including meditating, taking unsolicited court actions, and paying attention to signals that bring you back to the present moment. Continue reading and put into practice the advice given to learn to live in the moment.

Start with small steps. Even if you are tempted to revise your life completely, you understand that to start living in the moment; it is not necessary to overturn your way of life too much. Instead, start incorporating a new habit into your style at a time and, only when you feel you have made it your own, move on to the next. For instance, rather than meditate for 20 minutes on the first try, start meditating for no more than three minutes a day. Increase the time frame gradually, as you begin to feel more comfortable during meditation.

During routine activities, note the sensory details. Learning to live in the moment can be an integral part of the normal course of daily life. Being aware can easily be incorporated into your routine simply by highlighting the sensory details of your actions. Focus your attention on sounds, smells, perceptions, sensations, and images that derive from your habitual gestures. For example, the next time you brush your teeth, notice the scent of toothpaste, the noise emitted by the toothbrush that rubs against your teeth and the sensation that comes with it.

When your mind tends to wander, direct it wherever you want. It is normal that the mind tends to digress, but if you want to live in the moment, you need to keep it focused on the present. When you notice that your brain starts to wander elsewhere, hijack it again gently. Recognize the fact that you are distracting from the here and now without judging yourself in any way.

Do not worry if you notice that your mind starts wandering in the past or the future. It is normal for him to do it from time to time. Simply accept that you are taking a short vacation and bring it back gently in the present moment.

Choose a warning signal. In frantic moments, remembering to remain aware is not always easy. A signal of attention, for example, a thread tied around the wrist, a pen mark on the hand or a coin inserted into the shoe can help you remember to stay awake. Whenever you notice it, stop for a moment what you are doing and notice what surrounds you.

The signal of attention can also derive from the outside world; for example, the gesture of drinking a cup of tea, seeing oneself reflected in a mirror or slipping into shoes.

Over time you will begin to ignore the signal because you've got used to it. At that point, you'll have to replace it with another one.

Change your routine. Being overly routine may prevent you from being able to live in the moment. Changing your behavior is a way to be able to become more aware. You can opt for simple changes, for example by going a different way to go to work, changing the way you present yourself to people or slightly altering your favorite story. Often making small changes to one of your daily habits may be enough to make you more aware of the environment around you. Try to change direction during your evening walk or add a new ritual to the routine that precedes the moment of sleep.

Learn to meditate. Meditation is a great way to train the brain to live in the moment. When you meditate, you commit yourself to notice the thoughts that come to your mind and then simply let them go. Learning to meditate requires time, practice and valid guidance, so the best thing you can do is sign up for a course and rely on a teacher. If there are no lessons in the area where you live, you can rely on listening to a CD.

To take the first steps in the world of meditation, locate a quiet place and take a comfortable position. You can sit on a chair or a pillow, cross-legged. Close your eyes and focus on your breathing and while doing this, avoid being distracted by your thoughts. Let them appear and then move away. Without opening your eyes, look at the world around you. Pay attention to how you feel. What are you hearing? Do you smell anything? What do you experience on an emotional level? And on a physical level?

Set the alarm from the non-invasive alarm to know when to stop. The advice is to start with a short 5-minute meditation and gradually increase the practice time. Tell your roommates that you are meditating and ask not to be disturbed.

Be grateful for your expectations. Often having to wait for something makes us irritated, but if you want to live in the moment, you must learn to consider expectations as favorable occasions. When you are forced to wait for something rather than become impatient, be grateful for the time you can devote to observing your surroundings. Learn to consider waiting as breaks and appreciate the minutes at your disposal. For example, if you're waiting in line to buy your morning coffee, use that time to look around you. In doing so note the things, you feel grateful for when you are living.

Focus your attention on the part of your body. You can learn to be more in the present by focusing on the sensations you feel in a specific area of the body, for example, the soles of the feet. By shifting your attention from one part of the body to the other, you will learn to become more aware of the present moment.

If you feel that living in the moment is particularly difficult, close your eyes and concentrate all your attention on the plants of your feet. Note the sensations caused by contact with shoes or the floor.

Realize the curvature of the arch of your feet, feel the heels and the lower part of the fingers.

Smile and laugh more often. When you are in a bad mood, or you feel sad, being able to live in the moment can prove even more difficult, but a simple smile accompanied by a laugh, even if forced, will make you feel better. If you realize you are distracted by the present because you feel unhappy, try to smile and laugh at least a little. Even a fake smile and a silly laugh should be able to make you feel better immediately.

Be thankful. Showing gratitude helps you come back and stay in the present moment because it urges you to think about what you feel grateful for and to notice how it is affecting the here and now. Gratitude can also help you remember the many good things that are in your life. Learn to be grateful for the person you are, for how you feel right now and for everyone you care about: friends, family, and pets.

Take a moment during the day to recall something for which you feel grateful. You can express your gratitude aloud or choose to put it in writing to give it further strength. For example, you could say or write "I'm grateful for the sun that shines in the sky today, it's wonderful!" or "I'm grateful for the affection of my family, it's able to make me feel special."

Complete some kind gestures towards others. Performing unplanned kind actions will help you live in the moment because it will bring your attention back to what is happening before your eyes. Notice what the small gestures you can take to show yourself attentive to the needs of others are. Your kind actions will help you to slow down and give you the chance to see the world around you.

You could compliment a stranger, saying, for example, "I like her dress; it's very nice." In every situation, find a way to show your kindness. Even simple gestures like an open smile or a nod to the head can brighten someone's day and help you stay focused on the present.

Understanding Your Personality

We all have strengths and weaknesses, but the key is to focus on our strengths and minimize the impacts of our weaknesses. Learn to evaluate yourself and identify with your strengths and flaws. A simple assessment of your personality can help you understand the causes of undisciplined behavior and bad habits. Having an awareness of your personality helps you to manage your likely reactions to various situations to achieve the most favorable outcome.

Figure out the kind of person you are, your characteristics, what motivates and demotivates you. It will be easier for you to work on developing your self-discipline if you are aware of your behavior and its consequences. When you have a strong awareness, you will be more persuaded of the need to make changes in your life in order to achieve your goals.

Endeavor to act and conduct yourself according to the decisions geared towards achieving your goals, regardless of bad habits such as laziness, procrastination, or lack of resilience.

Identify your weaknesses and avoid distractions

Learn what motivates you and what can derail you. You can begin by learning about yourself and identifying your area of weakness and the distractions that can impede you from achieving your goals. Sometimes it can be very easy to indulge yourself in guilty pleasures that are not beneficial to your goals, so know the areas where your resistance is low and how to avoid those situations. For example, if your goal is to eat healthy then avoid visiting fast food restaurants and keep only healthy food in your refrigerator at home. If your goal is to reduce your social media consumption and time spent on your smartphone, then you can ditch your phone for a basic one or delete the apps or games which you are addicted to. As humans, we are prone to distractions, and it can be hard because of the role technology plays in our day to day life. Our phones and laptops are always filled with notifications calling our attention to information that might not be relevant to our goals.

When you remove the temptations, it becomes easier for you to stick with your plans and achieve your goals. The results of exercising discipline are success, self-respect, and a better life. "Mastering others is a strength. Mastering yourself is true power." - Lao Tzu

Practice self-denial. Self-discipline means saying no to instant gratification in favor of long-term fulfillment. To be successful, you must learn how to avoid indulging yourself and say no to some of your feelings, desire, and cravings. Train yourself to do what is right, even when you do not have a keen interest in doing it. Say no to alcohol some evenings. Reduce the time spent on social media; say no to junk food. Stop and think of the consequences before you act. When you exhibit self-restraint, you develop the habit of keeping things under control.

Your mind and body will do everything it can to resist change and growth. It's natural to feel lazy and undisciplined, but it is possible to overcome this weakness by determination and sheer willpower.

Go Above Feelings

The hardest part of becoming disciplined is maintaining the actions needed to achieve your goals. It requires constant hard work and fighting against comfort and instant pleasures. To do so, you have to separate yourself from the feelings that stop you like weariness, laziness or self-pity. You have to rise above them and make things happen, even when you feel tired, and stressed.

Successful business people also experience normal human feelings such as laziness and self-pity that are obstructions to achieving goals. But they found a way to overcome these feelings and focus. Laziness is actually your brain-saving energy for you. Moving from one place to another takes energy, and the brain is trying to discourage you from moving by sending body signals about how difficult it is to move. You are in control of yourself and should push your body to work and finish tasks.

"Rule your mind, or it will rule you."- Horace

Find an Accountability Partner

If we are sincere with ourselves, we will discover that excuses are avoidable lies that we tell ourselves to stay in the comfort zone and avoid the challenges involved in the process of achieving greatness. To prevent excuses, adopt measures to hold yourself to a higher standard and stop limiting yourself.

If you are accountable for yourself only, it will be very easy to give excuses and cheat. You can find someone to be accountable to. Get a friend or colleague with similar goals, workout partner, join a community with like-minded people or hire a coach. Hold each other accountable and monitor your progress. Do not permit excuses; make sure you praise and encourage each other when needed. This will create more motivation for you to follow through on your goals and accomplish them.

Whichever accountability system you choose, the aim is to take away your ability to make excuses and procrastinate; this enables you to follow your plan and develop a sense of discipline.

Its Goal Setting Time!

We've already established the significance of goal setting in the process of becoming a more self-disciplined individual. Thus, we can now work on setting those goals to improve productivity and increase your chances of success.

Productivity and self-discipline are two qualities that work in harmony, helping you to be a better version of yourself. You cannot have one without the other. Self-discipline keeps you productive while productivity further improves and refines self-discipline.

The Benefits of Productivity and Self-Discipline

Here are how these two traits are going to do you a world of good and give you a firmer grasp on why productivity is such an important trait:

Motivates Further Action

Deciding to become a self-disciplined person is a strong enough motivation to become more productive. You'll want to work much harder and go the extra mile.

No More Wasted Time

Procrastination is the enemy of success, and those without self-discipline often waste precious time that could have been spent working on bettering themselves or being more productive.

It Delivers Results

It's a wonderful feeling to see your labors and endeavors come to fruition. A productive person will almost always achieve what they have set out to do. Also, they often see the rewards of their hard work because they do what needs to be done to deliver results.

A Career Boost

No organization in the world would want to hire an employee who is not committed to working hard and is viewed as unproductive. Companies only want individuals who are committed to success, who are willing to do what is needed for the success of the business, and who is seen as an asset instead of a liability. If you lack productivity and self-discipline, your performance at work will slowly but surely start to suffer.

Essentially, when you have self-discipline and productivity on your side, you will be viewed as a valuable asset no matter where you go.

Setting Your Goals

Successful goal-setting should happen in 3 stages: Daily, Weekly, and Monthly. The shorter timeframe will allow you to evaluate and reflect whether the steps and measures which you are currently taking are leading you in the right direction. Smaller goals with timelines make bigger goals, and those short-term goals are often the small nudges that add up and push you to achieve your long-term goals. If anything, short-term goals prevent you from "setting and forgetting" your primary goals.

Phase 1 Equipping Yourself

Don't worry. You won't be spending a lot of money. For effective goal-setting, you'll only need to equip yourself with five types of tools: pens, paper, colored markers, sticky notes, and a vision board.

On your vision board, describe the ideal life that you see yourself living. Beside it, list the goals that you want to achieve. Throw in a couple of motivational quotes to help you get going. Your vision board will serve as the "The Big Picture" of everything that you hope to achieve. It will serve as the fuel to your fire. Once your vision board is done, you're ready to move onto the next phase.

Phase 2 Setting Daily, Weekly, and Monthly Goals

The goals you set for yourself need to be as personal as possible. These have to be things that you are aiming for, not what someone else expects of you. Personalized goals keep you enthusiastic, driven and motivated. The desire to reach these goals is what will keep you determined to stick to them no matter what.

Naturally, you should start with daily goals first, before working your way up to weekly and then monthly goals. Daily goals keep you on track and in the right direction to accomplishing weekly goals, which in turn aid you in reaching your monthly goals. Both weekly and monthly goals will help you stay committed on the path and can also serve as opportunities for additional goals.

To begin building effective daily, weekly, and monthly goals, here is what you need to do:

- Start with a basic daily goal: establishing a morning routine. Make this a habit that you can stick to, and one that will keep you organized and efficient as soon as you wake up in the morning. A morning routine can be as simple as making your bed every morning without fail. Remember, learning to commit to the most basic or simplest routines will make committing to bigger, more complicated routines easier. It is great practice for basic levels of self-discipline.

•	Set a morning routine for work too, where you would typically spend most of your time, next to your home. Your routines at work can include exercises that help you build and develop self-discipline. It can be as simple as adopting a more disciplined and productive mindset with even the smallest of tasks. Aim to stick to these routines every day. Another morning routine at work can include turning on your computer, making a cup of coffee, then settling into a create a task list of what needs to be done on the day and then responding to emails before jumping onto the tasks which require your urgent attention.

•	A weekly goal could be to take stock of your progress and environment at the end of each week. Has your environment helped inspire you to achieve your goal for this week? Or would some changes be necessary? Critically reflect upon your surroundings and make a note of the changes that need to take place. Remember to jot them down so that you don't risk forgetting about them later.

•	A weekly goal could also be making Sunday your day off. This day is when you would take care of yourself and recover from a week of hard work. Perhaps, it can even be a time to catch up with friends and family. That in itself is a goal too, especially if you have been guilty of neglecting the same in the past. It is important to maintain balance even if you are working to pursue your goals because when you feel happy and fulfilled, the desire to keep going is much stronger.

•	A monthly goal at work could be for you to organize your workspace. Tidying up can be done after reflecting on how well you did in achieving your work goals both daily and weekly, and then determining if your environment needs to be improved upon to increase productivity further.

Strategies to Help You Achieve the Goals You Set

Our different priorities in life will mean goals will vary from person to person. Thus, it's been mentioned that good goals should be personalized. However, the strategies that one can utilize are often very similar. The following strategies can help you better achieve the goals that you set:

Don't Do Too Much Too Soon

The key is to take baby steps, setting smaller, achievable goals that will keep you feeling motivated. Setting, and reaching, mini-goals is one of the best strategies you can employ. Each time you successfully smash through a goal, you will most assuredly have the desire to do even more because you want to feel that rush of positive emotions again.

One Goal Each Day

Even one goal a day will be beneficial. What you are trying to do here is to make goal setting and achievement a consistent habit. Make it a point to accomplish at least one thing each day, especially during the first 30 days. This time period is crucial to developing a habit. Once the initial 30-day period is over, this new routine will feel a lot more natural.

Be Flexible

Don't be too rigid with your goals. Learn to adapt and change with the curve balls that are thrown your way. Otherwise, you'll end up frustrated and stressed. Remember, no one can perfectly plan for everything and anything. The beauty of life is that it is full of unexpected twists and turns, and sometimes those curveballs could lead to even better things that we may not otherwise have had the opportunity to encounter. These moments are often called blessings in disguise.

Organization as A Form of Discipline

At this point, you can begin to write your schedule. Setting aside 6-8 hours for sleep, deciding when you will exercise (and what type of exercise), and eating only during certain timeframes is more than enough to get you started on the road to mastering self-discipline. Trying to change too much of your life all at once may lead to negative results. To become disciplined and stick to your schedule, it is recommended only to replace a few habits at a time. As you try to become a more disciplined person, your old habits (your old self) will do everything it can to keep things the way they are. Change can be very scary, and you have to realize that your subconscious does not know why you are trying to make these changes. To mitigate this subconscious fear, don't try to take on more than you can handle at once.

Waking up and going to sleep at the same set times on a daily basis is what the entirety of the rest of your schedule will depend upon. Eating only at certain times will not just help you to maintain your sleeping schedule, but also assist in being able to plan out the other positive habits that you intend on adding to your daily schedule. Getting regular exercise will help to teach your body when to store and expend energy, as well as even out the rest of your overall health. When combining these three principles into one schedule, you will be practicing the concept of organization.

Recall that the first pillar of self-discipline is maintaining a schedule. The second pillar is being organized. Being able to uphold your schedule will depend upon how organized your life is. If you are capable of eliminating the random, arbitrary, conditions of your life, then you will have a far easier time sticking to your schedule. These two pillars – scheduling and organizing – are absolutely necessary. Even more, they are also intertwined. One cannot be done without the help of the other.

You have to bring these two pillars together and create a solid foundation for your budding self-discipline to blossom. It is still recommended that you look through the other tips in this book, but you don't have to apply all of them just yet automatically. You should master these first concepts of eating at the right times, having a routine sleeping pattern before going to bed, and getting regular exercise before trying to add more good habits. If you can keep up these three things for 90 days straight, then they will have become habits, and you will automatically start doing them without having to utilize too much effort. After you have made all of these a part of your daily life, then you can begin to start practicing the other tips.

Yet there is something else you can do to expedite this process. You don't just want your schedule to be organized, but you will also want to begin practicing the art organization in other areas of your life as well. Take a look at the things you already do on a daily basis. Try to pinpoint what is redundant or unnecessary. If possible, try to remove these from your life. Adopt a mindset of not what you want to be doing, but what you should be doing. Before partaking in any activity that will require a dedicated amount of time, ask yourself if there is something else you could get done that is more important or beneficial. If there is, then do that instead.

Extend this notion of practicing organization to any area of your life that you can. When at work, is everything as organized as it could be? Do you know where everything is in your home without question? Do you have all of your bills in order and know when the next set of payments is due? Do you have all of your upcoming appointments written down and have allotted proper time to execute all of them? If you do not, then placing extra time aside and going through these items is mandatory. This is a very important point. To open up more room in your schedule, you need to first whittle down on the things that are taking up your time.

Cut down on the redundancies. Remove what is unnecessary from your life. Minimize your distractions. Design your schedule around the idea of doing what must be done first, along with setting certain timeframes for each activity. Follow your organized schedule for 90 days straight without interruption (or at least as few interruptions as manageable). The most disciplined people on this planet all stick to an organized schedule, and they don't have time for frivolous distractions. That is one of the great truths that are hiding between the twin pillars of self-discipline. For the disciplined person, not a single second of the day is to be wasted.

After successfully integrating all the advice given thus far into your life for 90 days straight, you may begin to add the other tips in the subsequent chapters into your schedule in any order you desire. However, there is one final piece to this first arc on the road to discipline that has to be explained.

Time Management

On the surface, this may seem like the same thing as sticking to a schedule. There are some clear-cut differences, but the concepts are intimately connected. The schedule is your cornerstone for achieving self-mastery. Using organizational skills and removing what is unnecessary are the tools that you use to construct your schedule. Yet, without proper time management skills, you won't be able to create a realistic schedule that you can live by. This chapter will tell you how to add these new, positive, habits successfully.

You may want to add some tools that help to make managing time easier. The most basic tool is the traditional calendar. Yet, our modern-day technology offers a variety of greater options. There are several different phone apps that are making logging time and sorting out your schedule a breeze. These are nothing more than digital calendars, but they come with all sorts of bells and whistles that make tracking time and remembering dates easier. Even if your schedule is not too filled up yet, you should look into adding some of these tools into your arsenal because there may be a time in the future where they will come in handy. Even if you don't wind up using them very much, the more options you have available, the more prepared you will be whenever life tosses you surprises. Trying to schedule your life in an orderly fashion can come with some pitfalls if you don't take extra care to make sure you have time for everything. The most common of these pitfalls is double-booking yourself. Pay attention to your calendar and use the modern-day apps to avoid doing this. Either way, add different items into your arsenal so you can plan for the future and organize your time more efficiently.

Another area that often becomes bloated and fills up time is sifting through emails. Along with this included is scanning phone calls. As you start to become a more efficient person, the value of your time will begin to increase, and you will have to practice proper discernment to maximize what time you have to offer to others. Electronic communication has become a standard way to interact with others, but more often than not, a lot of phone calls and emails are simply not that important. Set aside some time for yourself and go through your inbox and organize it according to priority. Whatever is not important can be placed lower on your itinerary, or you can simply remove whatever topics and conversations that are no longer relevant.

Do this with your phone as well. Go through your contact list and erase all the outdated conversations. If there are any archaic contacts, old numbers that don't exist anymore, or anything of the sort, you can remove them. Make sure to go through your voicemails and erase anything that is no longer needed as well. After your phone and email are cleared, you can start scanning the incoming messages before devoting too much time to them. Make sure that you read your emails in their entirety but also make sure that you don't spend too much time on conversations that don't need to be addressed right away. The reason you are taking the time to sift through your phone and emails is to open up space and prioritize whatever is most relevant to your current situation. Scan all your incoming messages and answer all of them in order according to priority. Whatever needs to be handled right away, get to it. Everything else can wait for the proper time they deserve.

When you are stuck waiting in a line at a store or sitting in an office waiting for an appointment, utilize that time. Since you aren't doing anything besides waiting anyway, why not go through all the messages that were placed lower on your list of priorities. In fact, any time you see yourself waiting for something (and you are free to use your hands) go through your phone and whittle down whatever pending conversations you haven't gotten to yet.

To the best of your ability, try to finish things as early as you can. Don't disrupt the most important aspects of your schedule, like exercise and sleep, but if there are any projects that you have to finish, it's best to get them done before the deadline is due. Handling things early is not only impressive, but it opens up more time to get to work on other things or pick up extra assignments. With that said, try to avoid being a perfectionist. If you are ever given a project to work on, it is recommended that you do the best that you can while working on it, but also know that when something is done, it's done. Being a perfectionist has both positive and negative attributes. The positive side of being a perfectionist is that whatever projects you hand in will be impressive and immaculate, but the negative aspect is that you may never finish anything at all. Don't fall into this trapping. Accept that some things will never be perfect, do the best you can, and move on to the next item that requires your attention.

Everything listed in this chapter has been mentioned to help you plan ahead for the future. That is the gift that time management can give to you. When you know where you're going and what you are going to do next, it will be far easier to remain disciplined.

The Strength to Say NO!

To remain disciplined, you must deny the disadvantageous. This, of course, relates to temptations and peer pressure, but it also relates to how you manage your time overall. You are going to have to practice proper discrimination – which means practicing proper discernment – which means telling people that your time is better spent doing something else then what they want you to do.

Becoming disciplined does not mean that you are going to take on the entire world. It does not mean that you are going to sacrifice your own betterment for everyone else. Becoming disciplined is an act of cultivating faith, courage, dedication, and wisdom. The whole point of constructing a schedule and utilizing the different exercises found in this book is to organize your time according to priority. Yet, there is no point in doing any of this if you are going to stop just to appease someone else. You are going to have to learn how to say "NO" to people. This may upset some of those around you, but that is a battle scar on the road to self-discipline.

Pay close attention to other people that are always jumping through hoops for others. Most likely, these same people live their lives in a circular pattern. The same problems present themselves over and over, and the same people step in to correct these problems. Don't be like this. Say "NO" to others. Let the world, and yourself, know that your time is valuable.

Of course, you will not be saying "NO" to everyone. You will be saying "YES" when a good opportunity presents itself, but "NO" to everything else. Proper discernment is not an easy thing to discover and practice. It is not something for the undisciplined person. It is only for those who respect themselves enough to know how valuable their time really is.

Saying "NO" can also help to increase confidence and self-faith. You don't need to impress everyone that you meet. Doing so would be a waste of time. You will only get in life what you put in. Use proper discernment to figure out where to invest your time in your life correctly. Have the strength to say "NO" to everything that takes up time and energy that could be used for more productive means.

How to Maintain Self-Discipline when Facing Adversity

Maintaining self-discipline can be challenging enough when things are going well, let alone when things don't go according to plan. Unfortunately, it's in the face of adversity that self-discipline must be maintained more than ever. After all, when things are going well, you can probably afford to put in a less than stellar performance from time to time and not suffer any consequences. However, when things are falling apart all around you, it is imperative that you maintain your highest standards at all times in order to stave off complete catastrophe. Fortunately, there are a few simple techniques that can help you to maintain self-discipline when facing adversity effectively. This chapter will reveal these techniques, thereby giving you the tools to keep your head above water in even the fiercest of life's storms.

Eliminate excuses

When you listen to post-game interviews in just about any sport, you will usually find that there are two types of interviews given by the losing coach. The first type and perhaps the most common is that which focuses on a multitude of excuses for why the team lost. More often than not the coach giving this type of interview will claim that the officials were unfair, the ground was in bad condition, the players weren't rested enough or any number of similar excuses placing blame on anything else but the team itself. While some of these reasons might actually be true from time to time, they are usually never the most significant reason for a team's defeat.

The other type of interview is that which focuses on reasons, not excuses. A coach giving this type of interview will usually accept responsibility for choosing the wrong tactics, making a bad choice regarding which players were picked for the game, or simply recognizing areas that the team clearly needed to improve upon in order to avoid such losses in future. In the end, this type of coach is the one who focuses on solutions rather than excuses and more often than not is the one who is more successful in the long run. In contrast, the coach who constantly provides excuses is the one who fails to accept mistakes made, meaning that he also fails to learn from them. Additionally, he will fall short when it comes to getting the best out of his players, meaning that both he and his team never achieve any significant level of success.

This scenario plays out in every area of life, not just in sports. Everyone, when facing failure, is forced to make a choice between owning the failure and ignoring it. Those who ignore it will claim that they weren't at fault in any way shape or form, rather it was a life that was unfair or specific circumstances that robbed them of the success they deserved. Needless to say, such an attitude prevents the individual from developing their skills in the face of adversity, meaning that they will probably fail time and again for the same reasons. In contrast, a person who takes responsibility for their role in a setback or defeat will learn a great deal from the event, enabling them to become better and stronger as a result. Subsequently, they won't repeat the same mistakes over and over again, meaning that they won't suffer the same failures repeatedly. In the end, such a person will achieve greater and greater success as a result of the setbacks they endure.

The trick is never to allow a setback to affect you personally, instead see it as a lesson to be learned. By treating setbacks as learning opportunities, you will grow stronger, wiser and more capable even when things go wrong. This means that you can make progress when others fall back or give up altogether. Such constant progress, even in the face of adversity, will set you head and shoulders above all the rest, especially those who require things to go just right in order to stand any chance of achieving success.

The Importance Of Avoiding Perfectionism And Procrastination

Another area where people struggle much of the time is the area of the 2 P's, otherwise known as perfectionism and procrastination. These two elements are polar opposites of each other, yet they have much the same effect on an individual in terms of keeping them from realizing their dreams. Every time a person engages in one or both of the 2 P's they invariably set themselves up for failure, thus robbing them of the success they so earnestly desire.

The first P, perfectionism, may at first seem like a good thing, something that everyone is seeking success should strive for. After all, how could it be a bad thing to try to be perfect? Simply put, any goal that is impossible is a goal that is self-destructive. Any time you set yourself a goal that you inherently know you cannot achieve you will lose heart right away, meaning that your efforts will be wasted since the outcome will never be what you hoped for. The fact of the matter is that life itself is imperfect. Circumstances are never perfect, people are never perfect and results, no matter how good they prove to be, are never perfect. Subsequently, when a person strives for perfection, they guarantee their own failure since you cannot create perfection from imperfect ingredients. This can only lead to frustration, guilt, anger and any number of other negative emotions that come from a person setting their standards far beyond reach.

This isn't to say that you shouldn't strive to be your best. Being your best, unlike being perfect, is something you absolutely can achieve. Therefore, it is reasonable to take inventory of all the ways that your efforts, circumstances and even results could have been better. Most of the time you will discover ways to improve your efforts and circumstances, thereby improving future results. Such constant self-improvement is critical for achieving any real and meaningful level of success. However, it is based on a healthy contemplation of what can be improved, not an unhealthy fixation on achieving perfection.

Another way in which perfectionism undermines a person's chances of success is that it leads to the second P, procrastination. If you wait for the perfect time to start a project, you will probably wait forever. It is a rare thing to find the absolute perfect time to do something. There will always be one or two elements within the timing that could be better, making any time less than perfect. This can result in you never getting started on a project simply because the perfect time to start doesn't exist. Furthermore, if you wait until you have the perfect circumstances, resources, people or otherwise, you will also probably wait forever. There can always be more money, better-qualified people, and better-quality tools, meaning that the perfect environment is always beyond reach. Only when a person is able to use what they have when they have it, can they forge ahead to create their own success.

This leads to the second P, procrastination. Like any other habit, procrastination becomes stronger and stronger the more it is practiced. When you put off a project for another time you create the sense that the project isn't worth doing, thus, the more you put it off, the less important it becomes until eventually, you won't do it even when you have no excuse not to. In the end, the more you procrastinate, the less likely you are to take action, meaning that you fall further and further away from reaching your dreams. The trick is only ever to put off a project when you cannot perform it due to a lack of resources. Even then, if you can do a small part of the project, it is vital that you do so. Any effort at all is better than no effort, as any progress is always better than stagnation.

Keep everything simple

Anyone who has dealt with planning in any form will know that the more complicated and complex a plan is the more likely it is to fall apart. This is usually due to the fact that most complicated plans focus on intricate details that can change at any moment. Rather than allowing for flexibility, such plans become rigid, causing progress to come to a halt whenever the slightest thing goes awry. In comparison, simple, flexible plans usually stand up to all sorts of challenges, proving more reliable as a result. This is because simple plans allow for adaptation to unforeseen circumstances. Subsequently, the simpler the plan is, the more likely it is to succeed.

One way to create a simple plan is to go one step at a time. Rather than plotting out an entire course that could go wrong at any moment, focus on smaller stages. This allows you to make decisions along the way that are more relevant to the circumstances that arise. By not being restricted to a complex plan you can adjust your course whenever necessary without fear of losing sight of the overall goal. This freedom to maneuver is particularly useful when things go so wrong that you need to scrap your initial plans altogether. The more open and simpler your plan is, the less you have to scrap in order to develop a new plan to accommodate the challenges you face.

Sometimes large, complex plans might be unavoidable. This is especially true in the event that you aren't responsible for creating the plan in the first place. You might find yourself given a large, complex task to perform, leaving you wondering where to start and which way to go. Fortunately, even in these circumstances, you can still create a simple plan with regard to how you tackle the bigger project at hand. The most effective way for doing this is to break down a large project into smaller, more manageable tasks. Each individual task will be simpler to perform, requiring less effort and time than the overall project. By breaking down large projects, you can better manage your time as well as your resources, only spending small amounts of each in order to accomplish the smaller tasks. This can also help you to measure your progress more efficiently seeing as rather than only having one deadline to follow you can create numerous shorter deadlines, each designed around the smaller tasks that make up the large project.

Another way that breaking down large projects can make all the difference is that it can prevent the procrastination that comes when a person is overwhelmed by the proverbial big picture. More often than not a person will put off starting a project that they simply feel unprepared to tackle. One example of this is painting a house. No one looks at painting a house as a simple, small task that won't be a problem. On the contrary, such a project will require a great deal of time, effort and money to achieve. However, if instead of tackling the project as a whole you break it down, focusing on one room at a time, suddenly it becomes more manageable and thus, less overwhelming. It is far easier to tackle the task of painting the bedroom than it is painting the house. Eventually, when each smaller task is completed, the big project will also be completed. This is how you can achieve those huge goals that seem beyond reach.

Make things fun

Finally, there is the all-important element of making things fun. Sometimes the simplest of things can make a huge difference in how you perceive a project or situation. For example, phrases such as 'deadline' and 'workload,' while seemingly harmless in nature, can have a highly negative impact on your morale. The trick here is to create your own vocabulary, one that is lighter and more fun in nature. This will turn even the most stressful of scenarios into something that seems far less sinister. An example of this is to replace the term 'deadline' with a word such as 'party time.' The chances are you will celebrate when you finish a project you are working on, so why not focus on that? When you use the term 'party time' you invoke a far happier image and emotional response than you will use such a grim term as 'deadline.'

Another way to keep things fun is to embellish the tools you use for work. This is particularly true with such things as calendars, planners and any other item used for keeping lists, dates and other critical information. When the information you reference is presented in a dull, uniform way, it can cause a certain amount of negativity in your mindset. This isn't to say that it will stress you out as such, rather it will simply leave you feeling as dull as the presentation itself. However, when you take the time to decorate such tools you can change your mood completely. By using bright, fun colors as well as pictures, funny quotes and the like you can turn a bulletin board into a board of inspiration. Now, whenever you look at critical information such as dates, meeting info and the like you will feel inspired and happy as a result of the fun way in, which the information is presented.

Finally, there is the aspect of celebrating milestones. All too often people get in a rut because their daily routine lacks any sort of celebratory moments to mark any progress made. No doubt you will make notable progress on even the most labor-intensive project each, and every day you work on it. If you only ever celebrate the final completion of such a project you essentially doom yourself to long periods of dull, monotonous days that lack any sense of fun and appreciation. However, if you take the time, even just a few minutes, to celebrate the small gains, you will keep yourself motivated in a way that will have significant repercussions. The simple truth is that the more appreciated a person feels, the more productive they become. This includes self-appreciation. Therefore, always take the time to mark even the smallest of achievements. After all, it's those small achievements that add up to create the larger, more noteworthy ones.

Challenges and Setbacks

Despite years of evolution, the human being is still plagued by animal instincts and driven by primal desires. These animalistic tendencies manifest themselves through harsh emotional reactions, and a man becomes an animal when he is unable to control these emotions.

These emotions are rooted in the evolutionary tendencies of a human being, in order to react appropriately to environmental stimuli. After millions of years, we have developed a complex brain that is capable of rational thought. This rational thought must be able to overcome all emotions so that the man can be his own authority.

In this chapter, we will discuss the possible setbacks. Traditionally, we have accepted that there are seven capital sins. In this chapter, we will not focus on the moral or spiritual implications of being a sinner. Instead, we will focus on the idea that these sins are in fact remnants of our animal ancestors. They are the crude emotional baggage that we must be able to control in order to push forward in our process of personal development.

Lust

This is generally related to sexual desire, but lust can also be the strong attraction we have to do something. For example, a good businessperson can be said to have a lust for business. By itself, lust can help you achieve something easily because it is synonymous with passion. However, if you let it take over you, lust can become an obsession. Historically, obsessed men have been seen as madmen, and they have been shunned by society. There is a difference between mad brilliance and madness, and sometimes the people who think they are only very passionate about something are in fact extremely obsessed about it.

The modern alpha male must be able to strike a balance between the overwhelming lust he feels for his goal, and a rational view of the bigger picture. In this day and age, the modern man is expected to be able to be in more than one place. The advancement of technology can be seen in one of two ways: either it has made everything more complicated, or it has made things connected and easier to achieve. It is a noble effort to be focused on one thing, but in the greater scheme of things, the man must be able to see that there are many other things going on in his life. Obsession will ruin him, and his connection with the real world. Letting yourself get devoured by lust will only destroy you and your connection with the people you love.

Gluttony

In achieving your goal, you must know when to stop. Historically, powerful warlords knew when to end their campaign. When a victory has been achieved, it is time to stop. Gluttony is the ravenous appetite for more and more, despite having enough. It is vital that you know when to stop.

Often, the cause of a gambler's addiction is what they call the "winning streak." Because they keep winning, they think that this streak will not end and that they will keep winning and earning more and more. However, when they suddenly get hit by an unfortunate blow, they might even lose everything they had. But because they had been winning, they will choose to block this out and keep going, losing more money in the process. A good gambler knows when to stop. Similarly, a man who has achieved what he needed to achieve must know when to move on to the next goal.

Envy

The difference between Envy and Jealousy is that a jealous person wants what another person has, and an envious person hates what another person was able to get. For example, it is jealousy when you say, "That man has a nice car. I want a nice car too. I wish I were that man." In contrast, it is envy when you say, "That man has a nice car. I should've had that car. I hate that man."

We all experience some form of jealousy in our lives because it is normal to compare ourselves to the better man. In the proper context, jealousy may even push us to achieve great things because we have seen other people achieve them first. If you see our friend succeed in the field of business, you might say, "I want to achieve the same success." And, once you act upon this jealousy, you will be able to achieve it too. So, jealousy can be used for good. However, when it turns into a bitter hatred, it becomes envy.

When you begin to hate another person for having something you don't, you begin to be envious. When you see another person reach your goal before you do, you might begin to hate him. This is wrong.

Hatred blinds people, and soon, you will lose sight of your own process and your own goal. It is good to know how others are doing, and a healthy competition never harmed anyone. However, when you begin to compare and destroy other people because you are envious, you will end up destroying yourself.

Simply accept that other people can be better than you are and accept that there are people who find it easier to achieve goals because they may have had the upper hand. Just go about your own path, because everyone eventually gets somewhere.

Envy goes both ways. Sometimes, you will find that other people are envious of you, and they will seek to destroy you. They may use niceness as a ploy to gain your trust and then they will use you and ruin you. You must be careful of these people. It is not to say that you must never trust people, but it would be wise to know how to read people. In the long run, knowing who to trust will help you reach your goals quicker.

Wrath

Strength is manifested in how a man controls his rage and how a man uses it. In society, we frown upon a man who is always angry. This man cannot be controlled, and he will wreak havoc on everything. We see this man as undisciplined. We see this man as a savage. After getting so far from our animal ancestors, we cannot become savages again. We must remember that we are civilized men with the strength to conquer our own anger.

Usually, anger comes from our own misunderstanding of a situation. It is a reaction to something that hurt us or whatever we hold dear to us. In defense of our honor or the honor of our loved ones, we use rage and anger to fight. Warriors backed into a corner facing nothing but death on either side have the advantage of having nothing to lose. So, they will use the rage they have of clinging on to life. Their fight is to the death, and they will not go down without proving their worth.

So, used well, rage is our desire to fight for the right reasons. Therefore, you must be able to find out if the reason you are angry is the right reason. As much as possible, controlling your own anger will allow you to think clearly and be able to see the point of view of your enemy. War strategists have all said that while it is important to understand your own strengths and weaknesses, it is equally as important to study your enemy. You must know how your enemy thinks. You must be able to read people well and see their point of view. In this way, you will be able to plot out your specific course of action.

Sloth

In the past, when explorers have set out to see the world and discover new continents, they experience what is called "doldrums." Doldrums is a state of stagnation when there are no waves, or there is no wind to push you forward. They will stay in the middle of the ocean, going nowhere. Their food would be depleted, and a lot of sailors have died of scurvy or hunger. There have been cases where they would begin to cannibalize on each other. Indeed, when put in a situation like that, the mind goes awry.

You must not let your mind go idle as doldrums, or else you risk going mad. When in the doldrums, you are doing nothing. You cannot expect the winds to change just because you wished it to. If you are a person in the creative field, sitting idle can cause the mind to create new stimuli, and this will lead to greater creative output. However, in order to do this, you must continuously be aware of your surroundings. You must be able to see the opportunities presented in front of you, and you must take them. Instead of just sitting around doing nothing, find a way to get out of doldrums so that you can move forward.

Greed

Being gluttonous means going on past the limit. Being greedy is to hoard without even needing the things you hoard. When you have a goal, then you have a purpose. You must know exactly what you need. You must be able to let go of the unnecessary while still being open to the possibilities. Certain things that you first saw as trivial and useless may, in fact, be useful, but there really are things that are just trivial and useless.

You must be able to let go of the useless. You cannot waste time collecting things that are impractical. Money, for instance, needs to be used. Misers hoard their money, and even though that makes them rich, it also renders their money useless. To a carpenter, a hammer is useful to be able to create something grand. But to a pilot flying in the sky, a hammer might just be sitting in the cockpit, taking up space.

All things have a purpose, and innovation means being able to see the purpose of things beyond the intended use. However, some things are just extravagant wastes. A man who is extremely rich, for example, might decide to waste his money on expensive cars and big mansions. One might ask, though: what does a man really need? What do you really need? Which things are necessary, and which ones are those you can do away with?

Pride

They say that the worst setback is this one. Pride is the false sense of greatness, a delusion of grandeur. You might think you are greater than everyone, but when you ask others, their opinion of you might be radically different. You must be able to see yourself as others see you, and you must be able to fashion your actions based on this. If you think you are so big and powerful, you might enter into something that will only make you fall.

There is a big difference between being prideful and being confident. Often, confidence means being authentic. It means being able to persevere despite the circumstances. Pride, however, means being entitled. A prideful person thinks that they are better than other people and that they deserve more than everyone without actually doing anything about it. This is wrong.

Conclusion

Thanks for reading this book. It's my firm belief that it has provided you with all the answers to your questions.

Now that you have read this book you have all the tools you need in order to create self-discipline in your own life. By establishing clear and achievable goals, you can begin to turn your dreams into reality each and every day. Furthermore, by ensuring that you remove negativity from your mind and your environment, you can increase the positive energy needed to achieve any goals you set for yourself. Finally, by taking the time to contemplate the principles of your self-discipline, along with how well your actions comply with those principles, you will increase the control you have over the choices you make and the way those choices affect your life. In the end, self-discipline begins with gaining control over your own thoughts and actions. However, as you increase your self-control, you will also increase your ability to control the circumstances around you. This is how the most successful people fulfill their potential. The very best of luck to you in developing your self-discipline, and thus creating the life of your dreams!

If you have found this book beneficial please consider leaving a review on Amazon as it really helps my work and in turn helps me reach others. Thank you.